THE MAN WHO LIVED IN AN EGGCUP

A Memoir of Triumph and Self-Destruction

The Man Who Lived in an Eggcup

A Memoir of Triumph and Self-Destruction

John Gamel, MD

Bascom Hill
Minneapolis, MN

CONTENTS

ACKNOWLEDGMENTS

I owe a debt to Rob Cohen, a gifted author and mentor who devoted many hours to my earliest efforts. Of all my supporters, Margaret Edwards remains the most devoted, tolerant, and long-suffering. An emeritus professor of English at the University of Vermont and a dear friend since high school, Margaret read a dozen of my short stories, and then delivered a painful message: the time had come for me to give up fiction and try my hand at a memoir. Without her guidance, my file drawer would contain nothing but rejection slips. A special note of thanks goes to Richard Burgin, who "broke the logjam" by publishing my first piece in *Boulevard*; with that credit in my cover letter, six more of my essays were accepted within a few months. Finally, there is my beloved wife Jessica Schumacher, whose eighty-hour work weeks sustain me in my career as a writer and a house-husband.

INTRODUCTION

My journey as a writer began in 1962, when I left my home in Selma, Alabama, for Harvard University. Here, within months of my arrival, I made a terrible discovery: I had nothing to write about. Worse yet, I suffered an attack of hypochondria so severe, it cast a suffocating pall over my life. To chase down my fear of illness and death, I became a volunteer at Boston City Hospital. In the end, this pursuit led to Stanford University, where I spent eight years as a medical student, intern, and resident.

The plan worked better than I had hoped. On the wards, my hypochondria gave me insights seldom available to a non-neurotic physician, while the life-and-death struggles of my patients soon drove my own fears into hidden regions from which they seldom emerged. Years of medical training toughened my hide, but in the end—dazzled by the aesthetic beauty of the human eye—I opted for the rarified world of ophthalmology.

As a professor at the University of Louisville School of Medicine, I fought blinding diseases for thirty years and published ninety articles in scientific journals. At the beginning of this millennium, my yearning to stray from the realm of science returned, but by now, a thousand triumphs and disasters had given me something to write about. The patients I best remember are those who would not be healed—men and women who fell victim to my ineptitude or to their own corrosive appetites. Each phase of my life told its own story, leading to a series of fifteen essays published in a variety of literary journals.

Now these essays have been melded into *The Man Who Lived in an Eggcup: A Memoir of Triumph and Self-Destruction*, which moves from the foibles of my youth to the more nuanced foibles of my later years. A warning to the faint of heart: much of what I report is gruesome indeed, but it is all true, and for every revolting scene, I conspire with my colleagues and patients to offer up at least one riotous blunder.

My narrative focuses on the emotional rather than the technical aspects of the doctor-patient relationship. Though I read and greatly admire such writers as Jerome Groopman and Atul Gawande, I leave to their skillful hands the task of showing readers the scientific achievements that define modern medicine. They speak eloquently of the damage done by insufficient skill or knowledge, but I would argue that harm often comes from a more treacherous source—the human heart.

CHAPTER ONE

The Man Who Lived in an Eggcup

David Johansen was never my patient, but his story became legend to every doctor, nurse, and medical student at Stanford Hospital. His year-long admission, which began with a three-month stay in the ICU, was followed by three months in transitional care and six months in rehab. He was in bad shape. His motorbike had run headlong into a parked car on El Camino Real, catapulting him into the middle of a busy intersection. Speed—of both the chemical and kinetic variety—was involved. Roy Cohen, the chairman of surgery, described David's injuries as "too numerous to count." No one knew how many vehicles ran over him before traffic finally ground to a halt, but the first patrolman to arrive at the scene reported that the truck whose rear wheel rested on David's right knee was loaded with six junked cars.

By the time they got him to the ER, his leg was coal black and swollen to the size of a tree trunk. Six weeks later, he awoke from a coma to discover that his leg, speech, and control of bowel and bladder were gone forever. A rehab nurse taught him to type with two fingers. The day before his discharge to the nursing home where he would spend the rest of his life, he typed a rambling commentary on his hospital stay. Most memorable was the closing paragraph: "In that wreck, I lost my leg, my voice, my bike, and my girl. Of these, the one I miss the most is my bike."

Though most amputees are devastated by their loss, David proved an exception. In the house of surgery, amputation inhabits the darkest room. Doctors are meant to heal, take away sickness, but the joy of healing is lost when this taking away carries with it an arm or a leg. Surrendering a nonessential organ—a ruptured spleen, an infected appendix, a stone-laden gallbladder—causes little grief, while the loss of a cancerous kidney or lung strikes a happy bargain with death. But the patient who loses a limb, however essential the surgery, will never be the same inside or out.

Even when chronic infection melts an extremity into a cumbersome mess, amputation brings with it a devastating sense of loss. Many of the Vietnam veterans I cared for at the Palo Alto VA hospital suffered years of agony rather than surrendering a mutilated arm or leg to the surgeon's knife. The chairman of orthopedics advised his residents to start their patients on antidepressants two weeks before an amputation, hoping to blunt the depression that often followed, on occasion so severe it led to suicide.

* * *

In the darkest corner of amputation's dark room lives an obscure operation, a procedure seldom performed but nonetheless horrific, an unspeakable mutilation of the human body. The operation's name—hemicorporectomy—tells its own story: in Latin, *hemi* means half, *corpor* means body, and *ectomy* means excision. The surgeon, hoping to cure a pernicious cancer or infection, severs the spine just above the pelvis and removes the pelvic bones with all their contents and appendages—the colon, rectum, bladder, hips, legs, and external genitalia—then wraps the remaining organs in an enormous skin flap. In the medical vernacular, this mutilation is known as "eggcup surgery," because any victim who survives the ordeal must spend the remainder of his or her life perched in a padded receptacle that resembles a giant eggcup.

I never met a patient who underwent hemicorporectomy, but George H., another Stanford legend, not only lived in an eggcup but did so—at least in part—of his own volition. His saga began at the age of nine when a car crushed his legs and spine and injured his brain. His spastic legs, drawn up behind his back in rigid disfigurement, made it impossible for him to lie on his back or sit in a chair. He seemed destined to spend his life lying chest-down on a gurney. By the time he was forty, weeping sores covered both mangled legs. Not that this handicap kept George confined to his room. Thanks to a large-wheeled gurney and powerful hands that spun those wheels like windmills, he was able to scoot himself all over Stanford Hospital. In the cafeteria, tables were moved to create an aisle wide enough for George's gurney, and here he befriended everyone he met.

At first it seemed strange talking to a man who lay chest-down on a gurney, resting his chin on one hand and gesturing with the other while his twisted, back-drawn legs formed a towering lump under the sheet. Yet day by day, George became less a disfigured victim and more an ordinary person, no different, in any substantial way, from those who sat around him. He had a mellow bass voice so much like Paul Harvey's that new acquaintances often commented on the resemblance. He read the *New York Times* from cover to cover and knew current events down to the last detail. And there was something more: an open face, iron-grey hair, bushy eyebrows, a warm smile, and a gentle, measured tempo to his speech that brought peace wherever he went. His one eccentricity was an aversion to conflict of any sort. Several times during the Nixon/Watergate hearings—they seemed to go on forever, one venomous debate after another—I saw George abruptly wheel himself away from a table when Nixon supporters and detractors began shouting at each other.

While admitted for a chronic infection in one of his twisted legs, George got bad news from Doctor Chase, the chairman of plastic surgery. Osteomyelitis had eroded the bones, leaving surgery as the only option. Worse yet, the infection had spread so far up the femur that a standard amputation would leave behind a festering core of antibiotic-resistant bacteria in the femoral head. For any hope of cure, Chase had to perform a disarticulation of the hip. This operation, also known by the unnerving titles hemipelvectomy or hindquarter amputation, would require complete excision of the leg and hip, leaving no trace of a stump, only the smooth curve of the pelvis.

George consented. What else could he do? After surgery, he disappeared from the halls of Stanford Hospital for several days. The next time I saw him, his gurney was parked beside the pharmacy counter while he chatted with an intern and two nurses. The lump formed under the sheet by the remaining leg had shrunk to half its former size.

"Good grief, George," the intern said as I approached, "you been doing speed or something?" Indeed, George seemed more animated than I had ever seen him. Propped on both elbows, his face aglow, he talked with boisterous energy, denying even a twinge of pain. Nonsense, of course; 120 stitches bound the massive raw wound on his hip. The surgery had gone splendidly, so splendidly George hatched a scheme: he would now persuade Doctor Chase to disarticulate his other hip.

"Jesus, George," the intern said. "That's a nasty piece of surgery." The rest of us nodded. We felt embarrassed. George was obviously manic, irrational. Perhaps decades of unrelenting pain had finally taken their toll. The intern said, "Maybe you could just get a regular amputation." The nurses and I murmured our assent.

"Not in a million years," George said, pounding his fist on the gurney. "Rehab says they can't fit me in a wheelchair long as that stump keeps getting in the way, and damn it all, I've put up with that rotten leg for thirty-five years. I want the whole goddamn thing off right now!"

We all stood silent, staring at the floor. I had never seen George upset or heard him curse. Surely it was the medication, the stress of the surgery. At that moment, four normal people—the two nurses, the intern, and I—shared a deep but helpless pity for the man who lay before us.

At first Chase wouldn't consider disarticulating a leg that posed no threat to the patient's life, but George harassed the poor man for months. Finally Chase sent him off to a psychiatrist, promising they would schedule surgery if George proved to be of sound mind. The psychiatry department was experienced in such matters; their faculty had examined candidates for the transgender surgery Stanford so famously pioneered. After the therapist declared George officially sane, Chase, true to his word, put him on the schedule.

* * *

The next chapter in George's story came from Freddie Tinsdale, an intern on the team that performed the second operation. The procedure went without a hitch. George woke from anesthesia cheerful as a new mother, refused his morphine, then violated his post-op diet by mooching a slice of apple pie from his roommate's tray. The next morning he wheeled himself down to rehab on his old gurney, where his smooth, legless pelvis was fitted for a special seat. That evening Tinsdale discovered George giving himself a bath. The nursing aides were meant to do that, but George had persuaded rehab to install parallel bars above his bed, and now, unencumbered by those useless legs, he could support the weight of his body with one ape-strong arm. Tinsdale pulled back the bed curtain to discover a naked, legless man dangling from a bar while he soaped his armpit.

On George's fifth post-op day, an even stranger thing happened. Late in the afternoon, the charge nurse on his ward paged the plastics team. Tinsdale, together with his resident and medical student, wandered up to find out what she wanted. Nothing much, the nurse said, just…well…somehow, George had disappeared. After lunch, he had rolled down to rehab on his gurney, eager to try out his new custom-made wheelchair, but the clerk on the rehab ward swore George had departed hours before. Calls all over the hospital—to the cafeteria, the ER, the ICU, the admissions desk—had turned up no sign of George.

How peculiar: a legless man gone missing. The nurse sat at the ward desk staring up at the intern, resident, and medical student. They stood in a circle staring down at the nurse. The hallway remained silent except for the overhead speaker. During the era before pagers or cell phones, it sounded every few moments: "Doctor Vinney, STAT to ICU…. Orderly with a wheelchair, Ward East 1A…. Blood bank tech, call extension 511…."

All eyes stared at the speaker.

"My God," the nurse said, "That's…. It's….Yes!"

The plastics team rushed down three flights to the basement, where two page operators were huddled in a cubicle. The team crowded around the doorway. There sat George, microphone in hand, perched in the new eggcup mounted in his new wheelchair. A set of earphones embraced his head. He leaned into the microphone and flipped a switch on the panel in front of him.

The voice was unmistakable: "Doctor Coursey, STAT to the ENT clinic." Finally George looked up and saw the doctors standing shoulder-to-shoulder in the doorway. His face glowed with delight. He took off the earphones, flipped off the microphone, and shouted, "My first job!" He clapped his hands. Tears streamed down his cheeks. "I've been on the payroll since one o'clock!"

The resident gaped in horror. The 120 five-day-old stitches that bound George's hip had held the weight of his torso for several hours. "Damn, George," he said, "get the hell out of that chair. You want to rip that wound open?" Then the resident went after the switchboard manager, but she insisted it wasn't her fault.

"How was I to know?" she said. "He'd been pestering me for weeks, rolling down here every day on his gurney, and I kept telling him I'd hire him soon as he could get in a wheelchair. He disappeared for a few days, then showed up bragging about his new wheelchair and asking when he could go to work. One of the girls was out on maternity leave, and the backup had broken her ankle at Tahoe. It only took me a few minutes to show him how to work the board."

The resident retired George on the spot, but two weeks later, Doctor Chase signed the release allowing him back to work. Five years later, when I returned to Stanford for a visit, George was still at it. He continued to live in an eggcup, bathing his half body every morning as it hung suspended over the tub, then swinging himself around his apartment on overhead bars and settling into his padded wheelchair.

For decades, he had cherished a fantasy—not the miracle of walking on his own legs but the simple triumph of caring for himself and earning his bread. At work, his voice was distinctive—a deep, soothing bass that put all who heard him at ease. And he was a smart man, knew every nurse and doctor in the building, knew all their routines, all their hiding places. Over the years, his dogged persistence interrupted many a tryst in the doctors' on-call quarters.

I have known many famous and many wealthy people in my life, but George is the only man I envy. I don't envy his eggcup, but I would give anything to own the triumph in his heart.

Chapter Two

The Doctor Is Sick

Vivian Kleinfelter was a thirty-nine-year-old patient with nineteen chief complaints. Her feet tingled. Her ears rang. She saw spots in front of her eyes. Gas pains kept her awake all night. Daily attacks of nausea were accompanied by cramps and rainbow-colored vomitus. All this had started with shortness of breath in her youth, attacks so terrible she sometimes fainted. Though a wise family doctor had taught her to control these attacks by breathing into a paper bag, the remaining symptoms had resisted the ministrations of a dozen specialists. It took me an hour and a half, but I finally got every last complaint scribbled down in her chart, together with her past medical history, family history, social history, and review of systems. Physical examination took ten minutes—normal head to toe, except for the well-healed scar of a biopsy on her left breast from three years before (a benign cyst) and a varicose vein on her left calf.

To the semiskilled eyes and hands of a third-year medical student, Vivian seemed the picture of health. Tall and solid, ramrod straight, with curly auburn hair, she had the figure and skin tone of a woman ten years younger. She talked on and on with the momentum of eager, well-rehearsed speech, her hands flitting about like hummingbirds as she touched the body part that harbored each complaint: eyes, ears, nose, throat, bosom, stomach.... But alas, her visit to the Stanford Medical Clinic came to naught. In the end, less than naught.

Alan Barbour, the clinic director, gave Vivian his best. He examined her body and reviewed every detail in her chart—including voluminous records from the Cedars-Sinai Medical Center in Los Angeles and the Pacific Medical Center in San Francisco—then delivered his diagnosis. He spoke with the deepest compassion, but the noble fellow insisted on telling the truth—it was all in Vivian's head, every symptom a hypochondriacal paradigm—and his efforts only enraged her. In the end, she stormed out of the clinic.

I called her at home three months later to find out how she was doing. "I'm better," she said. "A little better, since I saw an iridologist, and this aroma therapist in San Mateo gave me some essential oils—I sniff juniper and lavender with my right nostril every morning, then patchouli up my left nostril at night. They've helped a little. My ears don't ring as much, so I can sleep at night, at least when the gas pains let up, and my feet don't bother me like they used to. But that Doctor Barbour"—her voice rose to a shout, quavering with rage—"you can tell that son of a bitch to go straight to hell! All in my head! Why, I'd like to take his head and smash it with a hammer!"

Indeed, of all the hypochondriacs Alan examined during my rotation on his service, the poor man—a self-proclaimed specialist in hypochondria—never cured a single one. His intentions were good, his integrity unimpeachable, but the truths he told left dozens of patients grinding their teeth.

* * *

I know a lot about hypochondria, having suffered from it during much of my adult life—such a severe case that my search for a cure drove me to become a physician. The sense of my own mortality first came upon me during my senior year in high school, when Ed Miller, the brother of a close friend, died of Hodgkin's disease. Ed faded slowly—growing thinner and weaker each month, choked with phlegm, tormented by swollen lumps in his groin and armpits—but it was not until the end that his fate took on a personal meaning. I had seen death before: Mamaw, my beloved maternal grandmother, together with my father's parents and two great uncles. But they were old. Though I missed them terribly, especially Mamaw, their deaths had nothing to do with my own fate. Ed Miller was young, just three years older than I. His face haunted me—chalky white, the cheeks sunken, the eyes wide with confusion and terror.

My first year of college brought night sweats—an early sign of lymphatic cancer, or so I had heard—and an endless tossing about in my bed as every lymph node in my body throbbed like a boil. The doctor at the student infirmary was unimpressed. My temperature measured subnormal, and his probing fingers found nothing amiss in my groin or armpits. An agonizing three-day wait yielded a lab report that removed all doubt—no sign of disease.

I groaned with relief, slept soundly for a month or two, but then discovered a tingling sensation in my throat. Just a scratch, perhaps, but more noticeable day by day, gagging me with pain by the end of a week. A sore, maybe a festering ulcer, or…. Every swallow brought agony and waves of fear. A finger thrust down my throat discovered lumps at the base of my tongue. Again I fled in panic to the student infirmary. They referred me to an ENT specialist, a short, bald, light-footed man with a mirror on his head. He peered down my throat and laughed. I had discovered my posterior lingual papillae, normal structures located at the base of every human tongue and as nonmalignant as my nose and ears. My throat pain vanished, only to be replaced a few weeks later by a stabbing sensation beneath my breastbone that portended certain disaster.

My hypochondria ran a broken course. Some attacks came in the form of what one might call angst—an abstract fear, nameless and terrible, worse (how could that be?) than death itself. I fell into a frenzy when Comet Kohoutek was discovered in 1973. Despite astronomical assurances of a miss half the width of the solar system, I convinced myself this icy terror would smash the earth to bits. But more often my fear focused on an organ or two, a tumor that might spread to my lungs from a malignant mole, or a lump in my bowels that might soon invade my liver. Anxious fingers discovered a pulsating mass in the center of my abdomen. It was my aorta. One channel of my brain knew that each attack was nonsense, a false alarm no less absurd than all the others. But this was the weaker channel, too feeble to oppose the panic that tormented me when I woke during the night, my heart racing and my sheets damp with sweat. I needed more knowledge. More knowledge and—here, for once, my instincts served me well—a confrontation. I had to face down my fears.

* * *

Under Alan's guidance, the Stanford Medical Clinic became a hypochondriacal quagmire, a magnet for psychosomatic whiners from all over Northern California. I found Alan a wonderful man, a philosopher, and a devoted teacher. He was sixty when we met, semiretired after three decades of practicing internal medicine. During that era, every physician in America—except for Alan, or so it seemed—dismissed hypochondriacs from their practice as quickly as possible, but he was a pioneer, the noblest and most dangerous role a physician can play. Alan would be the first to heal those patients who did not want to be healed, a Don Quixote despised by his testy and vituperative Dulcineas. Short but striking in appearance, he had a large head, a long torso, stubby legs, and tousled iron-grey hair. The crinkly folds of age covered his lower eyelids. His voice was gravelly, his speech measured in long, rhythmic phrases.

"No one wants to be sick," he would say. "These patients just need to be shown that health will cure their loneliness, bring the affection they crave, and do it better than any imagined disease. Truth is their only hope."

I was young and inexperienced as they come, but my sense of pragmatism rebelled against this philosophy. It seemed like snatching a toy from a child because the toy is ugly. Who's to say a toy is ugly? This paternalism proved a disaster for Alan's patients. One couple in particular comes to mind, émigrés whom I nicknamed the Nabokovs: The husband, like the author, was both Russian and an avid lepidopterist. His wife suffered from a pain in her arm that had eluded diagnosis for more than a decade. They were an aristocratic pair, married for thirty years, trim and vigorous in their mid-fifties, with beguiling Russian accents and the poise of landed gentry.

They entered the exam room hand-in-hand, then gazed fondly at each other throughout the interview. The husband couldn't sit still. He patted his wife's knee, fidgeted in his chair, clasped and unclasped his hands, staring at Alan or his wife with watery, red-rimmed eyes. Alan set upon them with the skill of a master and soon rooted out the truth, not in the wife's physical exam or medical record—which revealed no sign of disease—but in the husband's tale of their nightly intimacies.

A pathetic tale, indeed. Though they slept in separate bedrooms, every evening brought an elaborate ritual: he wrapped his wife's ailing arm in a hot towel for ten minutes, then removed the towel, dried the arm, propped it carefully on three satin pillows, and covered it with an eiderdown comforter. He described with a gesture how he pulled the comforter up to her chin, leaning close to his wife and exchanging a smile of tender endearment.

"My darling," she said, laying a hand against his cheek, "you do take such good care of me." At her touch, the husband fell silent and stared at the floor.

"Do you kiss your wife?" Alan asked.

"Well…yes, well, of course," the husband said. A blush reddened his cheeks. "A kiss, a gentle kiss, of course, on the forehead." He spoke rapidly, as though hoping to outrun the embarrassment of further questions. "I come back several times in the night. The pillows shift, the comforter slides about, I must adjust them to assure that her sleep is not disturbed. I…"

"Do you make love to your wife?" Alan interrupted, leaning forward with elbows on knees to stare the poor man in the eye. The husband gaped. The blush on his cheeks grew darker. He blinked his red-rimmed eyes.

"I…we…of course, at our age…our children grown…"

"Has it been long? How long?" Alan's gaze was steady, his jaw set.

"Well…" The husband's face turned purple, like a man holding his breath. He wrung his hands. At last, with a sob of humiliation: "A few years, perhaps…perhaps ten. But at our age…"

"Let me tell you something," Alan said. "For her age, your wife is healthy as any woman I've ever seen. In my exam room a few moments ago, I watched her lean over and press her palms on the floor. And you—you seem to be in good shape."

"Yes, yes, yes," the husband gasped. "I play tennis almost every day, maybe two or three sets. Young men, college boys, sometimes they cannot beat me. I…"

"Can you achieve an erection?"

"I…well…yes, but…" The husband opened and closed his mouth. Silence. He and Alan stared at one another. At last the husband leaned forward, clutching the arms of his chair. "Why do you speak of such silly things? My wife is in pain, and you are meant to help her."

Alan gave his finest performance. He explained how their conjugal bliss had strayed from the path assigned by nature, fallen from the health and vigor of flesh-on-flesh embraces into the black hole of a cultivated illness. Would it not be better, more joyful and satisfying, to lift off his wife's nightgown rather than fiddle around half the night with a pile of pillows? Why not throw away that ugly toy—his wife's spurious pain—so the two of them could savor the pleasures of marital coitus? The Nabokovs received this wisdom in stony-faced silence. They missed their follow-up appointment and never returned.

Perhaps Mr. Nabokov needed his ugly toy. Perhaps the toy Alan wanted him to play with scared the poor man to death. Since Alan's pioneering efforts, hypochondria has worked its way into the mainstream. There is even a title—psychosomatic medicine—given to the treatment of those who will not be healed. Research on this subject has disclosed a tedious but reassuring consistency: though an occasional hypochondriac may fall down dead, he is no more likely to do so than a man of the same age who considers himself healthy. Which is to say, fear of disease, however troublesome for the patient or her doctors, has no effect on lifespan.

As for treatment, direct confrontation seldom works, and most specialists now recommend compromise and accommodation, avoiding any statement that resembles, "It's all in your head," substituting instead variations on, "Let's try this—many of my patients have found it helpful." Naturopaths, chiropractors, aroma therapists— an unending array of "alternative" practitioners—remain popular with hypochondriacs, while the purists who follow in Alan's footsteps by telling the raw truth have enjoyed little success. Truth is not beautiful when it steals a man or woman's raison d'etre.

* * *

No one rescued me from my hypochondria, a dark, suffocating cloud that cast its pall on the brightest skies of summer and threatened to hound me to the grave. Without radical therapy, my life would have dribbled away in a procession of fearful days and sleepless nights. The first glimmer of hope came from a related neurosis—my flying phobia. After one hand-wringing, knee-knocking flight, I noticed that my return flight a few days later aroused only a few sweaty tremors, while a third flight soon thereafter gave me just a twinge of nausea as the misty landscape unfolded six miles below. Repetition seemed to calm my fear of airplanes. *Hmmm*, I thought, *perhaps my hypochondria might also give way to a frontal assault. Rather than whimper like a coward, squirming in darkness and misery, perhaps I should chase down my dragon.*

I launched the first attack against my fear of needles. Needles terrified me, and a whiff of the isopropyl alcohol used to clean the skin sent me reeling. During my sophomore year of college, with trembling courage, I offered myself up to the Red Cross blood bank. The first few visits left me sweaty, light-headed, tingling in my toes and fingers, but eventually I mastered my fears, chatted with the phlebotomist, even watched the needle as it popped through my bluish skin into the swollen vein.

This therapy seemed to work, but my darkest fear had yet to be faced: hospitals, where patients, some even younger than I, lay dying from unspeakable diseases. I volunteered as an EKG technician at the infamous Boston City Hospital, a collection of ancient brick buildings connected by tunnels that smelled of urine and garbage. The wards stretched on forever, grey walls and high ceilings, twenty beds on each side of scuffed linoleum aisles. Even more daunting were the private rooms, sanctuaries reserved for the dying. Their doors were kept discreetly closed.

After a week on the job, I opened one of these doors to perform an EKG and found an enormous dead woman, but she was old. Later I glimpsed inside another private room as a nurse departed carrying a soiled emesis basin. The patient was a teenager with damp blonde hair, his face contorted in pain, a dark lump bulging at the angle of his jaw. The image burned itself into my mind. That night I tossed and turned for hours, my jaw throbbing until it seemed ready to burst.

But I persisted, seeking ever-more-gruesome sights. I peeked over a surgeon's shoulder at a belly filled with naked organs. An orderly allowed me to wheel dead patients, old and young alike, down to the morgue. My ultimate attack on hypochondria came during my senior year, when I applied to medical school.

* * *

Five years later, while an intern at the Santa Clara Valley Medical Center in San Jose, I glimpsed psychosomatic disease at its worst. Marguerite Sellers, a strikingly handsome woman, entered the ER on a quiet afternoon. Half the gurneys stood empty. As the two clerks sat dozing behind their desks, my fellow intern thought himself a lucky man when he opened the curtains around a gurney to find a patient who looked like Elizabeth Taylor. Marguerite had dark hair that hung down to her shoulders and desperate, convincing eyes. Even more convincing was her abdomen, a crisscross of angry red scars fringed by the tic marks of surgical closure, what surgeons call a "road-map belly." At the slightest touch, she moaned and tensed her muscles—the sign of a life-threatening abdominal hemorrhage or infection.

Marguerite told a compelling story, a tale for every scar: excision of a ruptured appendix, followed by abdominal surgery for intestinal adhesions, followed by an ectopic pregnancy in the right fallopian tube. Not such a run of random bad luck as one might think, since each of these disasters predisposes a patient to the next. Marguerite's belly impressed Sam Elmore, the surgery resident who examined her. In the hallway outside the ER, I heard him talking to Marguerite's intern.

"It looks bad," Sam said. "Six months ago, she had surgery for an ectopic pregnancy in the right fallopian tube, then last month she missed her period.

Now she's tender as hell on the left—a classic story for a second ectopic."

A second ectopic! My fellow intern and I sucked in our breath. An ectopic pregnancy occurs when an ovum, fertilized but misdirected, takes root in a fallopian tube and sprouts a false placenta shot through with fragile vessels. Rupture could come at any moment, causing massive hemorrhage, shock, or death. To our surprise, Sam didn't whisk Marguerite up to the OR. Instead, he inserted a catheter just beneath her umbilicus, then pulled back on the syringe, looking for any trace of blood in the abdominal cavity. The tap was negative, but that gave no real assurance. The false placenta could be the size of a lemon, growing larger by the hour, waiting to rupture and spill pints of blood into her abdomen. Sam admitted Marguerite to the ICU and ordered her vital signs checked every half hour.

A sad case, since her husband was on a business trip to Singapore, with no hope of phone contact, while all her other relatives had died. With no close friends, Marguerite would have to suffer alone. Alone indeed—flat on her back in the ICU, surrounded by comatose patients, listening to the rhythmic *clunk* of their respirators. The window by her bed looked out over a macadam parking lot. The ICU had no TV sets.

The next morning, when I stopped by the ICU to examine a patient admitted the night before, Marguerite's resemblance to Elizabeth Taylor made a stunning contrast to the corpselike faces of those around her. Though we didn't speak, her eyes followed my every step, as though she hoped to share her desperation with anyone who entered the room. Her loneliness lasted two more days, until Richard Burton arrived. That was the nickname the ICU staff gave Marguerite's husband. The charge nurse swore he was the handsomest man she had ever seen. In retrospect, it seems uncanny that Marguerite's illness should gather about it such abundant physical beauty.

Elizabeth and Richard reunited, with much shouting and waving of arms, though Richard spewed venom not at Elizabeth but at the charge nurse and every doctor in sight. Upon learning that no one had laid a scalpel on his wife, he lapsed into a crestfallen stupor, then wandered about the ICU mumbling apologies. His curse in life was to chase after Marguerite as she drove all over Northern California seeking a bizarre visceral redemption. During the past year, she had sold her story to three surgeons. Only Sam Elmore's restraint had denied her a fourth ecstatic incision.

I don't know what has happened to Marguerite since, but the prognosis remains poor. The curability of Munchausen syndrome—the compulsion to feign, create, or exaggerate an illness—ranks right down there with bulimia, pedophilia, and morbid obesity. It's likely that Marguerite escaped her husband's vigilance again, that other surgeons fell victim to her desperate eyes and her rigid road-map belly. Her husband explained that she had a PhD in nursing and for several years worked on an oncology ward at the University of Oregon. Few doctors can resist a patient who knows the right story to tell.

* * *

Marguerite gave me the wisdom to look into dark corners, root out terrible truths. Three years later, during my residency, this wisdom would serve me well when I cared for a patient named Mack Rae. A retired major general with the Strategic Air Command, he had piloted a B-52 Stratofortress on "hot" flights over the Arctic Circle. While his plane soared at 40,000 feet—carrying four hydrogen bombs, each addressed to a city inhabited by millions of people—Mack listened to his radio for a coded go/no-go command, thus assuring the most rapid possible massacre should war break out with Russia before his plane reached the point of no return. A cruel yet thrilling job, but old men are not allowed to do such things, so at age sixty Mack had to retire and resign himself to an ordinary life. But his life didn't remain ordinary for long.

Mack was always cheerful, especially when a new resident took over his case, since this allowed him to tell his story from start to finish. His beet-red eyes were blind, the corneas clouded by a greenish-yellow cast. Sticky mucous matted his lashes. I introduced myself, then remarked on the massive size of his medical chart.

"Can you imagine it, Doc?" he said, beaming with pride. "A man gets the tops of his eyeballs cut off. Then they have to go in there and take out his cataracts. His retinas fall off, they've got to be hooked back up—first one eye, then the other, then the first one again. Then they've got to cut off the tops of his eyeballs again, and damned if they don't get all scarred up just like the first time."

His chart listed several diagnoses: herpetic keratitis, secondary bacterial infection, perforated corneal ulcer, failed graft, secondary cataract, aphakic retinal detachment. Indeed, Mack's corneas had rotted away twice, but all attempts to culture herpes virus had failed, as had every treatment in *Duane's Textbook of Ophthalmology*. Drops and pills and injections gave no more benefit than so much tap water. Each complication had come in tandem with simultaneous onset and simultaneous progression in both eyes—evidence, or so it seemed to me, of a compulsive force.

Everyone rejected my theory. Even the corneal specialist balked, insisting that no one could do such things to himself, but he had not seen Marguerite's performance. Mack boasted of his suffering, his exciting new life. I asked him one day if he ever touched his eyes.

"Well, Doc," he said, "sometimes a man can't help himself. Just a little, every now and then. They sort of itch."

As he spoke, he held apart the lids of his right eye and rubbed the glaucous cornea with his index finger. The tip of the finger moved in vigorous circles, spiraling outward from the cornea onto his boggy, inflamed conjunctiva. The sight shocked me; a normal cornea sends out waves of searing pain at any but the lightest touch. Then Mack closed the eye and rubbed it with his knuckle, rubbed until the violence of his gouging sent chills down my spine. The swollen lids made a wet, sucking sound. A strand of mucous oozed from the tear duct. "Ah, that feels better," he said, and began rubbing the other eye. This time, the mucous squirted onto his cheek.

Of course I couldn't be sure. Perhaps Mack didn't know what he was doing. Perhaps all that scarring had left his corneas no more sensitive to pain than the soles of his feet. But the smile on his face, even as his knuckle squeezed mucous from his tormented eyes, suggested a man in the throes of ecstasy. Perhaps this was the ecstasy denied him when—day after day, year after year—he could never unleash the four thermonuclear treasures nestled in the belly of his B-52.

During my career, I met others whose craving for self-destruction proved more precious than vision—indeed, more precious than life itself.

CHAPTER THREE

Asphyxia

I was only a few weeks into my career as a medical student when I saw naked lungs for the first time. Stanford's tedium of labs and lectures was meant to endure for two years, but the curriculum committee decided to spice up our schedule with an occasional hands-on clinical experience. Thus, early one morning I was dispatched down the Bay Shore Freeway to Santa Clara Valley Medical Center in San Jose, where I was gowned and masked and led through the *whooshing* pneumatic doors of an operating room.

The air reeked of peculiar substances, the names and purposes of which I would soon come to know: Phisohex, an antiseptic soap redolent of banana oil; Betadine, a tincture derived from iodide; isopropyl alcohol, a skin prep used before inserting IV needles. In the center of the room, beneath piercing overhead lights, stood an oblong mound covered with blue surgical drapes. In the center of the drapes lay a square of human flesh—the patient's shaved and sterilized chest, darkened by the burnt-umber tint of the Betadine.

Professor Huett, my assigned mentor, stood across the OR table from an intern and a third-year resident. The professor and I introduced ourselves to one another, then watched the resident split the patient's breastbone from sternal notch to xiphoid process with a circular saw. The whirling blade made the same high-pitched whine one might hear in a carpenter's shop, but instead of sawdust it cast a line of soupy pink marrow onto the drapes. The bone itself, heated by the friction from a hundred razor-sharp teeth, smelled like burning rubber and overcooked meat. I had grown up in Alabama, where gutted carcasses hung from many a tree during deer season, but this was different. This was *human* flesh. A surge of nausea prickled my scalp with sweat.

The resident laid the saw aside, inserted a chrome-plated spreader into the wound, and twisted the handle until the edges of split bone gaped over a dark linear hole. With each twist, the wound spread wider. The ribs cracked. The hole gaped one inch, two inches, three inches. A final twist gave a final, resounding *crack*. The OR fell silent except for the rhythmic *hiss...clunk...hiss...clunk...hiss...clunk* of the respirator. Doctor Huett peered down into the pulsating cavity.

"Nice job, son," he said, giving the resident a nod. "You split that sucker right down the middle."

Above his surgical mask, Huett had close-set green eyes and a towering forehead crowned by a blue paper cap. I adored the man the instant I heard his slow Georgia drawl. Here was a true Southerner, a professor of surgery, no less—my first encounter with a fellow redneck since arriving in California.

"What we have heah, Doctah Gamel," he said, peering through a set of half-glasses perched on his long, thin nose, "is an oat-cell carcinoma 'bout the size of a peach. We'll have to wait for the frozen sections to be sure, but y'all can take my word for it, this baby's an oat-cell all day long. There it is, wedged in beside the mediastinum."

The patient's lungs lay deep within the shadowed cavity. Normal lungs are soft, pink, filled with diaphanous sacs, but these were coal-black and stiff as leather. I knew they were lungs only because they rose and fell with the hiss of the respirator and cradled between them the beating, vein-laced heart. Professor Huett let me touch the tumor with my gloved finger. It felt like a rock.

The case went on for a long time. Just before noon, the resident lifted the black lung and its clinging black tumor out of the chest and handed them off to the scrub nurse. An hour later, the sternum bound tight with five twists of bone wire, Huett and the resident rushed from the OR, leaving the intern behind to close the skin. In the locker room, they tore off their masks and paper caps, threw their gowns into a laundry hamper—exposing lean freckled arms and curly chest hair peeking above the collars of their blue scrub shirts—then hit the door of the doctors' lounge like lions after a kill. They flung themselves into folding chairs set around a table littered with ashtrays, paper plates, dirty knives, a box of saltines, an open jar of peanut butter. The aroma from a pot of tomato soup boiling on a hotplate brought saliva to my mouth, but my colleagues were seized by a craving more primal than hunger. I heard the crinkle of torn cellophane and the *tap tap tap* of a pack against a palm as two unfiltered Camels inched their way out the open end.

"Lawdy, it's almost one o'clock," Huett mumbled, the unlit cigarette bobbing up and down between his lips. "We were stuck in there damn near five hours."

A match cracked and flared. He took an enormous drag and held it deep in his lungs. He smiled. His eyelids drooped with pleasure. His nostrils gave off jets of smoke as he hummed *mmmmmm*. He took another drag, then— with a delicate mastery of lips and cheeks and diaphragm I had never before seen outside the Deep South—blew the smoke slowly out of his mouth, sucking every wisp up his nose in two elegant streams.

"A hell of a case," he said. "Mah back hurts."

The resident, a handsome fellow with pale lashes and curly yellow hair, mumbled "Un-huh," then took a drag so deep his cheeks caved in, pressing so tightly against his teeth I could count his molars. After a few more ravenous drags, the inch-long ash on his cigarette fell to the floor.

* * *

My dear Uncle Melvin, a prosperous lawyer in the oil-boom town of Hobbs, New Mexico, was a wise and generous man. He saved me from a lifetime of manual labor in lower Alabama by sending me to prep school, supplementing my college scholarship, and paying my tuition during the first year of medical school. But alas, the poor creature was hopelessly addicted to food, liquor, gambling, and cigarettes—a true omniholic. There were rumors of loose women in his past, but by the time I knew him, his ponderous belly and failing lungs had removed infidelity from the list. At his peak—immaculate in a Panama hat, white silk suit, and black wing-tip shoes—he was round as a bowling ball. His legal skills earned him $800 a day, a princely sum at the time, but he had the self-control of a termite. When his wife bought a Sara Lee cheesecake during one of my visits, Melvin ate only one thin slice at the dinner table, but thoughts of that creamy treasure tormented him until—over the course of the evening, skulking again and again to the refrigerator—he had eaten the last crumb.

Every workday at four p.m., Uncle Melvin closed his law office to head for cocktails at the Mesa Lounge. By dinnertime, his round face was cheerful and pink. Late one evening, thick-tongued, deep in his cups, he assured me, "There's nothin' in this world better'n four good friends'n four quarts of Kentucky bourbon." All night long his violent snores rattled the house. He never missed a day of work, but at the breakfast table, his bites of soft-boiled egg quivered on the spoon. The morning paper rustled in his unsteady hands. During jaunts to Las Vegas, he played dice and roulette and blackjack. He played until dawn, so avidly the MGM Grand Casino gave him a complimentary suite. When his estate was settled, his assets—including major stock in four oil wells—were all but consumed by a mountain of debt.

Yet Uncle Melvin's final undoing came from a passion more corrosive than dice or cheesecake or bourbon on the rocks. I witnessed this passion full-on, right in the face, one afternoon at the Lee County Courthouse in Hobbs. It was the last time I saw him alive. My visit was meant to celebrate his recovery from a bout of pneumonia that had kept him in the ICU for two weeks, the fifth of five near-fatal bouts scattered across an emphysematous decade filled with coughing, wheezing, and racking fits that drowned out the Sunday sermon and left Melvin purple in the face. But now he was reformed, recovered, not a pack in the house. He hadn't touched a cigarette since his discharge from the hospital.

"You don't need to tell anybody about this," he said. We were standing alone in the stacks of the courthouse library. A moment before, there had been a whisper in the librarian's ear, a furtive gesture as Uncle Melvin slipped a cadged cigarette into his shirt pocket, and now, in a long, dim corridor lined with books, he held the flaming match with a steady hand. Off liquor for six months, thanks to a peptic ulcer, he had lost thirty-five pounds. His white silk coat sagged between his shoulders, but his cheeks were still round, his lips full, the lower lip dark and pendulous—the pink face of an overgrown cherub.

Melvin took a deep, sensual drag, crossing his eyes to focus on the smoldering tip. His barrel chest heaved as the smoke rushed into his lungs, straining the fabric of his white shirt. He coughed violently, fist to mouth, *hack-hack-hack*, bowing lower with each *hack*, until, bent half to the ground, a gasping breath shot him bolt upright. Again, *hack-hack-hack*, lower, lower, gasp, bolt upright. With each spasm came rales, rhonchi, phlegm in the tubes, a warbling crescendo of blats and whistles from the mucous-filled sacks deep in his lungs. The veins in his neck swelled out thick as fingers. His eyes bulged, his face shaded, moment by moment, from lavender to mauve to indigo to midnight blue. Beyond endurance, seemingly beyond survival, the attack rocked him to and fro in a writhing fit of suffocation. By the end, his face was black, his bloodshot eyes bulged from their sockets. At last his breath settled into a morbid wheeze. His cheeks slowly faded to their usual cherubic pink. He wiped his mouth with a handkerchief.

"I've got to get rid of these things," he said, his voice husky, full of rattling, phlegmy overtones. "They're not doing me any good at all." He stared at the cigarette smoldering between his fingers—a searching look, a gaze that spoke of astonishment, eternity, the confusion of a child in pain. He took another drag.

Perhaps it was Uncle Melvin's fate that begat my fascination with voluntary asphyxia. During medical school, poring over anatomy, pathology, histology, and physiology, I learned the basics: of all human tissues, the lungs—loaded with 300,000,000 alveoli, delicate sacs whose membranes span an area the size of a tennis court—offer the most vulnerable target to caustic agents. Attacked by smoke and tar, the alveoli thicken, bulge, and rupture, merging into blebs that whistle like flutes and croak like frogs in a midnight pond. Asthma adds fuel to the fire, causing spasms that block the bronchioles. At the first whiff of smoke, the few surviving alveoli choke off, forcing the victim to pay for each drag with a suffocating convulsion.

At the personal level, these minutiae translate into a simple proposition: hold a pillow against your face and keep it there forever, pressing a little harder every day.

* * *

On the respiratory ward of Santa Clara Valley Medical Center, half the patients were "sitters"—so short of breath they couldn't lie down, even for an instant. They slept every night sitting up: nodding off, waking, tipping to one side, nodding off, slumping, waking, exploding now and then in a coughing fit as they waited for dawn to bring another day of breathless misery. The rest of our patients were mostly "in-betweeners"—those whose bouts of pneumonia or acute bronchitis carried them a step further along the road to suffocation but whose lungs, still harboring a few islands of pink scattered among the black scars, allowed them to sleep lying down. The chief of pulmonary medicine took a dim view of the whole business. He insisted that within five minutes of discharge, in the car on their way home from the hospital, most of the sitters and 'tweeners would be sucking on a cigarette.

* * *

In Mellow Dee's, a stucco-fronted lounge across the street from Valley Medical Center, an alcoholic leans his elbows on the bar and looks down with jaundiced eyes at the bourbon in his glass. There are bandages on his arms, covering punctures left by the intravenous needles withdrawn only hours before. His throat is raw. The Sengstaken-Blakemore occluder—a tube thrust down his throat, anchored inside his stomach with a balloon, then inflated to twice the thickness of a garden hose— plugged his esophagus for six terrible days. It saved his life, staunching the esophageal hemorrhage caused by his shrunken, rock-hard liver, but now every swallow brings waves of agony. He lifts the glass, tips it gently side to side, savoring the rich bouquet of the liquor, the *clink* of the ice cubes, and the faint whorls of melting ice as they lace into the amber liquid. He sips. A fiery pleasure rushes down his raw, swollen throat. Then, slowly, the precious molecules seep into his bloodstream, carrying their balm to his patient, long-suffering brain.

Booze is a stern taskmaster, but it allows its acolytes time, a few hours of golden glow before fate holds out her hand for payment. Smokers like Uncle Melvin have only a few seconds: one puff—suffocation. Melvin lived every hour wheezing, coughing, struggling to climb a flight of stairs, but he put that cigarette between his lips, and with one quick drag bartered away the last breath in his devastated lungs. And he wasn't alone but one of thousands, tens of thousands, who smoked themselves right to the end of emphysema's merciless road. Evidence, I would argue, that nicotine trumps heroin, knocks speed and crack cocaine into a cocked hat.

* * *

Wilma O'Malley was a fabulous patient: the queen of asphyxia, the bravest of women, an institution unto herself. Almost everyone with emphysema gives up smoking at least once, surrendering the evil weed for a week or a month or—rarely, alas—forever. Not Wilma. Her integrity was unimpeachable. The only time she surrendered a cigarette was when an ambulance attendant snatched it from her blue fingers or an intern rammed an endo tube down her trachea. For a decade, her calamitous body taught the doctors at Valley Medical Center more about asphyxia than a library full of journals.

Wilma was forty-seven years old, a scarecrow with a prune face and streaked iron-grey hair, but she could have passed for sixty. The bluish cast of her skin matched the color of her eyes. But that was at her prime. Under duress, as her remaining alveoli choked off one by one, she darkened to purple, then blue-black, then—in the final throes of suffocation—pitch-black. Her emphysema had progressed slowly, with miraculous languor, allowing her iron constitution to survive oxygen starvation that would kill almost every mammal on earth. Though her arms and legs were sticks, congestive heart failure brought on by the struggle to pump blood through those scarred lungs had caused her feet and ankles to swell up like dough-filled balloons.

When Wilma came to our ward, her man was never far behind—a tall, cadaverous, bronze-skinned fellow of uncertain nationality who stood silently beside her bed for hours at a time. We nicknamed him the Mummy. No one ever heard him speak. Every admission followed the same script: Wilma rolled in sitting bolt upright on a gurney, gasping and wheezing and coughing until she vomited into an emesis basin held beneath her chin. While the Mummy hovered in a corner, the charge nurse grabbed the denim satchel that lay on Wilma's gurney and rifled its contents—a toothbrush, a coiled half-empty tube of toothpaste, a flannel nightgown that smelled like an ashtray—all the while ignoring Wilma's breathless protests: "Bitch!...*wheeze*...*hack hack*.... Don't you dare...*wheeze*.... I got my rights...*hack hack hack*... *wheeze*.... I'm gonna call..."

Finally, stuck to a greasy, newspaper-wrapped sandwich, Wilma's stash was found—a bag of cigarette butts scavenged from public ashtrays. After the nurse seized Wilma's poison and tucked her into bed, I thrust an endo tube down her trachea. A respirator pumped oxygen and aerosolized epinephrine into her lungs. An IV dripped Lasix and prednisone and antibiotics into her veins. At last, as dawn began to break, I stumbled to my own bed, leaving her alone with the *hiss...clunk...hiss... clunk...hiss...clunk* of the respirator. Slowly, as the drugs took effect, the bronchospasm gave way. The surviving alveoli perked up. Her complexion faded from midnight purple to the purplish translucency of a peeled grape. At rounds a few hours later, her hungry eyes waited for me. They followed my every move. She was alive, alive but wretched, tormented by a heartbreaking need—where was her precious nicotine?

Day by day, her arterial oxygen inched its way up. When it finally reached a level that might sustain life in a seal or a porpoise, we had to pull the endo tube, leaving her trachea unguarded. Then the Mummy came from nowhere, stealthy as a ghost. He had a talent for invisible locomotion. We never saw him walking, but a nurse would look up to discover his silent form looming over the ward counter, or an aide would find him lurking in a shadowy corner of Wilma's room. No matter what precautions we took, a bag of pilfered butts soon found its way beneath Wilma's bedclothes, and she began puffing away. After each drag, she concealed the smoldering cigarette between her mattress and the wall.

Wilma assured me cigarettes had nothing to do with her ravaged lungs. Raised in the Blue Ridge Mountains of Tennessee, she had spent her childhood in a dirt-floor shack, inhaling smoke and creosote fumes from a Franklin stove.

"That's what tore up my lungs," she insisted. "Since then, I ain't never quit coughing. Back home they call it smoke blight. Breathing that stuff just ruint me. Then there's that mutt I call Tootsie Roll, some kind of rat terrier. He sleeps in my bed every night. I'm allergic to the beast; he chokes me up something terrible, but what can I do? Tootsie's better company than any man alive. Cigarettes, they ain't never hurt a bit. You doctors keep going on and on, but you don't know squat. Nothing relaxes a person like a puff ever' now and then."

I was not a good doctor to Wilma. If the chief of pulmonary medicine had known the truth—the ugly, unnatural truth—he would have given me a black mark on my report. When I entered Wilma's room, I looked her in the eye, casting nary a glance at the plume of smoke snaking its way up from the hidden cigarette. Day by day, without either of us speaking a word of this matter, the subterfuge fell away, until I sat by her bed with her chart in my lap, chatting for ten or fifteen minutes while Wilma smoked at her leisure. The Mummy stood motionless in a corner of the room, his face inscrutable, blank as the wall behind him.

Where did it come from, my indulgence of Wilma's corrosive habit? My mother smoked three packs a day for fifty years, smoked until her fingers turned yellow and her sheets reeked of tar. A disastrous parent—bitter, vindictive, on occasion breathtakingly cruel—but my mother nonetheless, with a stubborn mouth and a squint-eyed smoking style much like Wilma's. Was this indulgence a vicarious tribute to the loved but dangerous woman who bore me? Or a nostalgic return to my childhood in the Deep South, where parishioners strode into church exhaling their last puff, where sand-filled ashtrays lined the halls of every hospital, where a pall of grey smoke hovered near the ceiling of every restaurant in town?

At Wilma's bedside, I watched in fascination as her vice worked through its cycle. She did not suffer the ambivalence that tormented Uncle Melvin. When she looked at the cigarette smoldering between her fingers, there was no uncertainty in her gaze. No doubt. No hesitation. Her eyes shone with a moist brightness. This was her life, her meaning—her *lover*.

After a few drags, her skin turned dusky and her thin blue lips quivered as they pursed around the soggy butt. She gasped, wheezed, coughed. Then, between coughs, with a wink and a nod and a face that grew darker every moment—"excuse me...*hack hack hack*...*gasp*...*wheeze*...for...*hack hack hack*...*gasp*...*wheeze*...a second..."—she turned on the Bennett respirator beside her bed. The motor whirred. She clamped the nozzle between her teeth and closed her lips around it, holding the cigarette aside with her free hand. As the Bennett forced in breath after breath, aerosolized epinephrine blasted open her spastic bronchi. Oxygen soared into her capillaries. Her complexion faded from deep purple to powder-blue. She took the nozzle out of her mouth. The coughing was gone, the wheezing faint and intermittent, subdued for the moment by the massive dose of epinephrine.

She took another drag.

Three drags later, her face almost black, she was ready for another refreshing pull on the respirator.

* * *

Except for the lucky few delivered by Caesarean section, we are all born asphyxiated. I delivered a dozen babies during my internship, and you can take my word for it: when that round, button-nosed face pops out between its mother's thighs, the skin is blue, the eyes squeezed tight in the agony of suffocation. How else could it be, with the chest and umbilical cord trapped in the iron grip of the birth canal? Long before love and honor, before power and strife and cruelty, even before mother's milk—breath. Newborns suck in air like a tidal wave, suck in precious lungs full, then scream with the ecstasy of oxygen, scream to tell the story of their violent, suffocating birth. We breathe, and life begins.

Oxygen is the ultimate addiction, the craving that never goes away. At Pearl Harbor, after Japanese torpedoes capsized the battleship Oklahoma, all but thirty-two of the 400 men trapped inside were drowned. When divers worked their way down to the flooded midshipmen's head, they found a nightmare—six upside-down toilets, each containing a bubble of oxygen-free air and the face of an asphyxiated sailor. At the moment of certain death in rising waters, those six men fought for their last breath. I remembered them as I watched a veteran of Utah Beach whose larynx had been removed the week before. He grimaced. Tears of frustration ran down his cheeks. He was struggling to smoke through his tracheostomy, but the cigarette was too small to make a tight seal with the tube in his throat.

Medicine has given insight into the human heart. I have witnessed the devotion of parents to their children and the tender bond that binds husband to wife for decades on end. Yet when a jaundiced alcoholic—days after a near-fatal hemorrhage, his belly still swollen with ascitic fluid—sentences himself to a blood-vomiting death by pouring more whiskey down his throat, I have to wonder: is such self-destruction not evidence of the greatest passion, the greatest devotion of all?

* * *

Wilma died the year after I finished my internship. I never pitied her. Weaklings like me have no right to pity her. We tiptoe through life, clinging to our tiny pleasures, skirting every vice that threatens the peaceful descent into a nursing home we cowards so deeply cherish. Wilma had the guts to go after what she loved, eager to pay pleasure's price every waking moment of every day. I tried a few serious drugs during my youth, but in the end, my courage failed. I smoked two packs a day for three years, then quit the day after Bobby Kennedy's assassination, thanks to a vicious attack of bronchitis.

Now, instead of smoking cigarettes, I eat bran, lift weights, ride my bike fifty miles at a clip. I drink six ounces of gin every night and would like to drink a lot more. My internist sighs with envy when she reads my lipid profile. And yet, in the midst of my seventh decade, on certain vague fall evenings, I feel a surge of resentment. Where is the ecstatic purpose to my life, a purpose so raw and precious I would endure suffocation to possess it? Perhaps I will live twenty years longer than Uncle Melvin, hounded to my grave by the nagging suspicion that he had more fun than a wimp like me can ever imagine.

CHAPTER FOUR

Spinal Beauty

What a difference a day makes. On March 31, 1971, I was useless. Supernumerary. Tits on a boar hog. Which is to say, a medical student. The next day, the state of California gave me a license to practice medicine, and the Santa Clara Valley Medical Center gave me three starched white jackets with *DR. GAMEL* stenciled over the heart in blue ink. Immediately beneath, in the more durable medium of embroidery: *INTERN*. The pockets held my stethoscope, reflex hammer, tuning fork, and visual acuity card—gifts Eli Lilly hoped would encourage me to prescribe their excellent medications. Now I could sign my own orders. When a patient stopped breathing, it was my problem.

I had finished medical school three months early, hoping to lie around and drink a little beer until my internship started in July, but an intern in the class ahead of me skied into a tree during his vacation in Tahoe. He broke ten ribs, lacerated his liver, and tore his right kidney from its pedicle. A phone call from the chief of staff at Valley Medical Center caught me in a weak moment, lounging on the dilapidated porch of my rented cottage, halfway through a seedy joint cadged from my next-door neighbor. The chief gave me a sob story about his interns working forty-eight-hour shifts to fill in for the Tahoe casualty, who wouldn't be back on the job for at least three months.

Six days later, refreshed and optimistic, I shook hands with Harvey Fitzgerald, my junior resident, a scrawny man with a narrow jaw, caved-in temples, and wild, straw-colored hair. There were dark circles under his eyes. He looked me over, taking in my fresh face and my fresh white jacket.

"God, you look good," Fitzy said. He laughed and squeezed my shoulder. "That won't last long."

* * *

The odor given off by an E. coli abscess leaves a licorice taste in the back of the throat. A No. 11 Bard Parker blade is razor sharp, angled for deep penetration, encouraging the pus to pour out in warm yellow dollops. I trotted down the world's longest corridor to a staff restroom, leaned over the toilet, vomited copiously, spat, coughed, and cleared my throat. I turned around to find Fitzy standing behind me.

"So, kiddo," he said, "maybe you should be a drug rep." I turned back to the toilet and spat two or three more times. He handed me a gauze pad from the pocket of his white coat. "Got some on your tie."

Fitzy's humor never let up. He made an amusing but stunningly crude remark when the breast of a large corpse flopped over the edge of a gurney as it bumped down to the morgue. He poked an overweight nurse in the umbilicus and asked when the baby was due. He gave nicknames to everyone in the hospital. Two jaundiced patients on *B* ward became the Little Lemon and the Big Lemon. Liver disease had ravaged their bodies, leaving both with bony chests and wasted limbs, but ascitic fluid had swollen the Big Lemon's belly to the size of a beach ball. On the private wing, we had two GI hemorrhages, the Good Bleeder and the Bad Bleeder, distinguished one from the other by their skill at using a bedpan. The four Frat Brats were scattered around the surgery floor—two in the Surgical Intensive Care Unit, one in the Transitional Care Unit, one in the ortho ward. On the Bay Shore Freeway, they had ended their spring break at Chico State by tucking their car under the rear axle of an eighteen-wheeler.

Two Frat Brats departed during my first week. Brat One, a pin in his femur, stretched out on the back seat of his father's Lincoln Town Car, while Brat Four rattled down to *M* ward on a gurney with the sheet pulled over his head. Fitzy said, "One gone high, t'other gone low." Under the sheet, Brat Four looked pretty good—a little pale, a blood clot in one nostril, an NG tube dangling from the other. The chief pathologist insisted we send our corpses down with every tube and catheter in place. Perhaps we had killed the patient by poking something into the wrong organ. That left us with Brat Two's persistent coma and Brat Three's punctured lung.

Then there was the Bone Woman. All cancer patients tend to waste away, but her body was a walking skeleton even before she began coughing up blood. Every two hours she made a pilgrimage down the hall, shuffling along at a snail's pace, her various attachments—the cast on her arm, the IV pole, the drooping IV line—all rocking back and forth with the rhythm of her slippered feet. Her floral-print gown hung open. On her chest, above a useless brassiere, she bore the mark of death—a radiation portal tattooed in red ink. Even an intern could read the story: lung cancer had spread to her arm and cracked the bone. She smelled like an ashtray. I stared in fascination at the tar-stained fingers, the wasted legs, the tiny, eager steps that inched her toward the smoking lounge.

Passing her room one afternoon, I heard someone sobbing, "Oh, mother...please...please...." Through the doorway I glimpsed a red-faced man leaning over her bed. Apparently he convinced her she might cure her cancer by giving up cigarettes. At rounds the next morning, she thrust her bony hand under the bedrail to grab Fitzy's arm.

"Doctor, I'm gonna quit," she said. "Tomorrow for sure. I swear. The whole carton in the trash."

Fitzy squeezed her hand, looked her in the eye, and gave his warmest smile. Her coarse hair was dyed brown, the grey roots an inch long. Her face showed every hollow and ridge of the skull beneath. The eyes lay deep in their sockets.

"No ma'am," he said, holding her hand with both of his, leaning down until their faces almost touched. "That won't be necessary."

The Bone Woman died five days later. The next morning, her room lay clean and fresh, the sheets drawn tight, waiting for Spinal Beauty to arrive.

* * *

A day went on for a long time. Twenty-four-hour shifts followed eighteen-hour shifts. We walked down corridors filled with shadows and faces—vivid faces, bloated or wasted, jaundiced, cyanotic or chalky white, each according to their disease. We walked on coffee-colored linoleum, beneath bare overhead pipes—red for steam, blue for water, black for sewage that gurgled every time a toilet flushed. We walked alone or in slow, murmurous, down-gazing teams. Venetian blinds covered the windows of the charity ward. The private ward had pink drapes. Every night, janitors mopped the floors. At one, two, three o'clock in the morning, I heard the clank of their buckets, smelled the pine scent of their detergent.

"Doctor Gamel, I have a patient for you."

It was Mrs. Stizel, the bed-control supervisor. She sat alone, exhausted, the peak of her white cap showing above the *B* ward counter. Her face was pale and soft. Untidy grey hairs curled from beneath her cap. Fitzy called her Grandmamma. Her voice was coarse, throaty, deep as a man's. "The blue team is overloaded," she said. "We must ask the red team to accept a transfer."

She forced a smile. Her hand rested on a thick chart divided into sections by labeled tabs: *History*, *Physical Examination*, *Laboratory Reports*, *Progress Notes*. On the front, in bold black letters: *CATHERINE MARY KOHLER—VOLUME III.*

In what had been the Bone Woman's room, I found a girl with a twisted torso, her sternum thrust up like the prow of a ship beneath her flannel gown. The clear mask of a nebulizer covered her lower face, delivering oxygen and moisturized air with each breath. I had expected these things. The chart said a seventeen-year-old Caucasian female had severe kyphoscoliosis with secondary pulmonary compromise. The lungs don't work when the spine is bent like a pretzel. Now she had pneumonia, hypoxia, and tachypnea—thirty respirations per minute. But the chart said nothing about her face.

What was Cathy's secret? Was she beautiful? Not really. She had a long nose, a little broad at the tip. Except for the nose, her face was angelic, expressionless as a doll's, framed by carrot-red hair that lay spread across her pillow. Mist from the nebulizer settled in fine droplets on her cheeks and eyelashes. She had indigo lips, translucent skin, the bluish tint of suffocation. Mostly, though, I think it was her eyes—pale green, wide-set, elusive. A desperate child, she struggled for breath every moment, but her eyes never pleaded. They never looked at me. They never looked at anyone.

"Hello," I said. "I'm Doctor Gamel. You've been transferred to my team. How do you feel tonight?"

Nothing doing. Her eyes remained fixed on the TV screen above the bed. A minute went by before her gaze flicked over, took in my white-jacketed form standing by the bed, then flicked back to the screen. The room filled with laughter as Lucy swung a rubber chicken over her head and chased Ricky around a grainy black-and-white kitchen.

The next morning, Fitzy and I stood beside Cathy's bed while he asked the usual questions. How had she slept? Did she have any pain? Was her breathing better? Each reply, muffled by the nebulizer, gave off a puff of mist: "Fine. No. Yes." Fitzy pulled the curtain around the bed while I untied three bowknots down the back of her gown, exposing cyanotic skin, a spine that curved and twisted, thrusting her right shoulder into a pale blue hump. Her breathing was rapid, strident, frantic. With each inspiration, the skin on her flanks sank into furrows between the ribs. Her breath sounds came through my stethoscope as from a great distance, the whisper of a desperate, faraway struggle.

I laid her down and palpated her abdomen, the narrow, scaphoid abdomen of a girl, no wider than the span of my hand. A tuft of pink lint nestled in her umbilicus. Her eyes never strayed from the screen, though most of it was blocked by the drawn curtain. Afterward, as we stood in the hallway outside her room, Fitzy said, "Stubborn little brat," but he was the one who named her Spinal Beauty.

Later that night, I stopped by Cathy's room, clutching a thin chart labeled *CATHERINE MARY KOHLER— VOLUME IV*. The lights were on, the TV droned, but she lay asleep. Beneath the plastic mask, her parted lips showed the gleam of white teeth. Tiny droplets clung to her long, innocent lashes. She smelled like baby powder. Her arms, covered with downy, copper-colored hair, lay folded on her chest. I turned off the lights and the sound on the television, leaving the screen alive so she would have something to watch if she woke in the night. The bluish-white glow played across her face. Her struggling breaths rose and fell over the hum of the nebulizer.

* * *

The interns' call room was lighted by a dome in the center of the ceiling. I pulled the string, lay on the bunk, and dropped into sleep like a brick down a well. A man who craves sleep craves nothing but sleep, envies no one but the peaceful, comatose patients. Sometimes the phone rang four or five times before I could remember where I was. One night a Filipino nurse shouted, "Doctor, Doctor, come quick, patient dying!" and hung up. Five wards, a hundred odd patients under my care for the night, and my only clue: "Doctor, Doctor, come quick, patient dying!"

Surgical ICU—a lucky guess. Frat Brat Three sat bolt upright in bed, a beautiful boy with wide-open eyes, bushy dark hair, a halo of sun-bleached ends. Blue lips. Blue fingernails. Rapid, desperate breaths. The boy was suffocating, terrified, his eyes following my every move as I stripped off his flannel pajama shirt and pressed a stethoscope against his chest. The left side was silent. The overhead lights pierced my eyes. I struggled against the stupor of darkness and sleep. My mind said *pneumothorax*, but that was the end of it. *Pneumothorax. Pneumothorax*? How long did I stand there looking into those wide-open eyes, eyes that said, *This isn't nice, Doctor, not nice at all—no matter how fast I breathe, it doesn't help.*

I watched my fingers peel a bandage from his flank, exposing a clear plastic tube threaded between his ribs. The tube was clamped shut, streaked with bloody serum. The day before, Fitzy had thought the boy's punctured lung was healed and ordered a nurse to disconnect the tube from the vacuum pump. Fitzy was wrong. My fingers removed the clamp, connected the pump, flipped the toggle switch. I was startled, wakened, by a wet, glutinous sucking sound, the rhythmic *glub-slurp-glub-slurp-glub-slurp* of an enormous infant nursing an enormous teat.

Unseen, deep in the boy's chest, his lungs filled with air. He sighed. His breathing slowed. The duskiness faded from his skin. Under the bright fluorescent lights, his chest and arms glowed with an olive tint. I helped put on his pajama shirt. He slumped against the pillow, closed his eyes, sighed again. I pulled the covers up to his chin. He turned on his side, smacked his red, dry lips, then fell asleep.

A few days after the boy's discharge, I got an impassioned letter from his mother in Malibu Beach. She thanked me in flowery prose for saving her son's life, but by that time, I had forgotten his name. To tell the truth, I had probably never known it. The fruit of his mother's womb, more precious to her than life itself, but to me he was Frat Brat Three, a nineteen-year-old Caucasian male treated for a traumatic pneumothorax and sent home with a thumb-sized scar between his fourth and fifth ribs. Someday a girl, caressing the smooth olive skin of his flank, would feel the scar beneath her fingertips. "Oh, my," she would whisper, her breath warm in his ear, "where'd you get that?"

* * *

The Big Lemon died, followed three days later by the Bad Bleeder. Frat Brat Two was taken off the respirator and dispatched to a nursing home for the remainder of his comatose life. Fitzy celebrated the Little Lemon's seventy-eighth birthday by hauling the old woman out of bed, summoning every nurse and orderly on the ward, and putting his arm around her shoulders to lead the group in singing "Happy Birthday." Early the next morning, the Little Lemon began screaming her head off. She screamed for six hours, the arching spasms of a woman in labor, until the gallstone no one knew about passed out her common bile duct. Her jaundice cleared. A few days later, on her way to the discharge desk, the scrawny, wrinkled, nut-brown woman leapt from her wheelchair and grabbed Fitzy around the neck, kissing him on the lips until he broke her grip to keep from suffocating. This was his payback for the "Happy Birthday."

* * *

Fitzy's touchy-feely routine fell flat with Cathy. She didn't pull away when one of us took her hand, but the hand just lay there, cool and damp, lifeless as a dead fish. Our gentle touch, our kind voices, our caring smiles— all came to naught. Her eyes never budged from the TV screen. Only a grunt or a single syllable ever came out of her mouth. Her twisted body had twisted her psyche:

ignored, rejected, taunted for years, she had hardened her heart against human touch.

But I didn't give up. On rounds one evening, I took a gauze pad from the pocket of my white jacket. Every time Cathy exhaled, mist from the nebulizer settled in fine droplets over her face, her lashes, and her lovely red hair. While Fitzy went through his questions, I dried her face with the gauze, then gently brushed a few strands of damp hair from her forehead. It worked. Those pale green eyes, glued to that wretched screen for a week, were mine at last. She looked at me. The room seemed to flood with light. My reward had come at last—a gaze so piercing it took my breath away. Cathy lay silent, entranced, while Fitzy's questions fell on deaf ears. A torrent of meaning soared through the empty space dividing me from this lonely girl, a torrent that spoke of pain and cruelty, of a fathomless need that had lived for years on end without hope or a single tender moment.

Fitzy saw what was happening and winked at me. I had made contact. As we turned to leave, I heard a faint voice behind us. Perhaps it said, "Thank you," or, "That was nice," but by the time I turned around, it was too late. *Ted Mack and the Original Amateur Hour* had sucked those pale eyes back to the screen. At rounds the next morning, I would discover them fixed, glued, stuck to that execrable TV with more tenacity than ever, as though my precious breakthrough had only stiffened her resolve.

But in the hallway, fresh from our victory, Fitzy choked up. His lips trembled. He put his arm around my neck and whispered in my ear. Had I seen volume one? No, I hadn't. What volume one?

"You lucky bastard," he said in a hoarse voice. "I wish I'd never looked."

Fitzy led me to the deserted *B* ward counter and hauled it out of a drawer—*VOLUME I* of Cathy's chart, a bound four-inch stack of papers: nursing notes, lab reports, physician's orders, vital signs, all recorded during her early admissions for asthma and pneumonia. Near the front, Fitzy showed me ten black-and-white photographs, each calibrated by a vertical ruler along the left side.

The first photograph showed a little girl standing naked beside the ruler with her back to the camera. She was 4'3" tall, her buttocks white between crisp tan lines. Someone had parted her long hair down the middle and pulled it forward across her shoulders to expose every inch of skin, then marked the vertebral points along her spine with thumb-sized black dots. The dots showed a mild *S*-shaped curve running from her cleft to the base of her skull.

The second photograph showed a child 4'7" tall. The curve looked worse, but only a bit. With her clothes on, Cathy would have seemed a healthy child, but year by year the curve grew steeper, until the last photograph showed a cruel black snake tilting the pelvis and contorting the ribs and shoulders into ugly, painful angles. Her skin, hidden from the public eye, was pale, unmarked by tan lines. Her hair was ragged and badly combed. No one pets a twisted child.

Fitzy and I sat side-by-side at the ward counter. The lights dimmed. It was ten p.m., the ward silent except for the distant hum of a refrigerator in the drug room. Beyond the counter stretched the faint yellow glow of corridors dappled with shadows, lined on both sides by the doors behind which our patients slept. I caught a whiff of pine oil. An unseen mop clanked in its bucket.

I closed Cathy's chart. Fitzy burst into tears, pressing his hand against his mouth to keep from making too much noise. He cried for a long time, slumped with elbows on knees, blowing his nose on gauze pads and lobbing the soggy pads into a trashcan. I put Cathy's chart back in the drawer. Neither of us spoke. We rose and went our separate ways.

I had lost my heart to Cathy even before Fitzy showed me *VOLUME I.* It happened soon after her transfer to my service, when I entered her room during evening rounds. Here was the bouquet of hospital life—Lysol, isopropyl alcohol, the urine of a diapered comatose alcoholic in the room next door. I turned off the overhead light and turned off the sound on the TV, leaving the light from the flickering screen to play across Cathy's sleeping face. As I watched the rise and fall of her chest under the flannel gown, there came a special treasure. Her eyelids quivered. Her legs twitched. The sheet fell away, exposing a pale, slender foot. She whimpered, tensed her body, and pulled at the oxygen tube, lifting the nebulizer to show, for an instant, the indigo blush of her lips.

What colors filled the dreams of this blighted child? Did sleep show her wildflowers, dark, secret pools, the icy flakes of a winter storm? Did minarets rise up to pierce a blue morning sky alive with butterflies and iridescent clouds? Her vulnerability, her desperate needs—oxygen, epinephrine, antibiotics, endless attention to detail—weighed upon my shoulders like the cloak of a king. I sheltered her. I sustained her. This was what I lived for.

* * *

What magic binds a doctor to his patient? Something happens, an emotional spark like the spark that binds mother to child. We doctors try to give our best to everyone, but some become precious to us. They steal our hearts.

An eighty-year-old Caucasian woman, deathly pale and hairless as an egg, awaits the last hours of her pancreatic cancer. While I sit by her bed filling her chart with my left-handed scrawl, she touches my shoulder. "You've got it all wrong," she whispers. "They're not teaching you young doctors a damn thing." When I ask what she means, she replies in a voice so faint I must cup my hand to my ear: "You're holding that pen in the wrong hand." Her fragile, tremulous smile has stayed with me to this day.

A ninety-four-year-old Filipino veteran of the Spanish-American war is admitted to the Palo Alto Veteran's Hospital. In his room, I find a wasted lump lying under the bedclothes. He seems comatose, so I speak to the woman standing at the foot of the bed, a dark-eyed Filipino beauty who looks twenty years old.

"Are you his granddaughter?" I ask. My guess is a great- or a great-great-granddaughter, but I'm playing it safe.

"Oh, no," she says, "I'm his wife."

"His *wife*!" I shout.

"Yes, his fourth wife."

"His *fourth* wife!"

During the silence that follows my outburst, a laugh ascends from the lump in the bed. A muffled laugh, faint but full of life, full of a final, glorious triumph that shines in my memory. He dies three days later.

However much we love them, sooner or later our patients always leave us. I lost Cathy to the knife. The first hint of her fate came when Fitzy got in a shouting match with Ernestine Shoemaker, the chief of Physical Medicine and Rehabilitation. I saw the two of them striding toward the PMR conference room, both frowning and red in the face. After the door slammed shut, I couldn't hear what they said, but they made lots of noise.

Later Fitzy told me the story. Shoemaker was an excellent doctor, adored by her patients, but with colleagues she had a clangorous way of making her point. Fitzy nicknamed her the Linebacker. A short, stocky woman, she wore her dark hair cut like a helmet, and her shoulders bulged under her white coat. Fitzy said it was all flab, but an orderly on PMR swore he had seen her heft patients out of their wheelchairs with her bare hands.

Shoemaker wanted some big cheese up at Stanford to cut on Cathy, slice her back open and implant a titanium rod to straighten her spine. Fitzy flew into a rage. The operation sounded like a horror show. We hunted down the chief ortho resident, a big Dutchman named Jansen. He showed us horrible pictures in *The Archives of Orthopedics*—skin flayed, muscles stripped down to the bone, the spine a row of white knots. The next page was worse—pliers, screwdrivers, huge gloved hands, a titanium rod running down the middle of a bloody mess.

"My God!" Fitzy said. "They'll kill her."

"Well, yeah," Jansen said, "that happens. They lose tons of blood. Sometimes the spine breaks, they have to abort the procedure. They did the first few cases in Paris, and a couple of patients ended up paraplegic. It just depends."

Shoemaker wouldn't listen to reason. The battle raged all the way up to Valley Medical Center's chief of staff. They even called Jansen to examine Cathy, and he jumped ship. "Do it," he said. "It might kill her, but it might help." What nonsense. Nobody asked me. I thought the debate would go on for weeks, but three days after it began, Mrs. Stizel called from behind the *B* ward counter.

"You missed the show."

"What show?" I asked.

"The big hullabaloo. About an hour ago, two guys in funny uniforms"—ambulance attendants sent from Stanford, as it turned out—"trotted down the hall with a gurney, grabbed Cathy, and hauled her off. You would have thought she was being abducted. I followed them down to the discharge desk, and when the supervisor tried to hold things up because of the paperwork, Cathy sat up on the gurney and cursed her, cursed like a sailor. Holy heaven, I never thought I'd hear words like that from a grown man's mouth, much less a girl's. They finally got things straightened out, but just as they wheeled Cathy off to the ambulance—I swear, you wouldn't believe it—she spat at that supervisor. Just puckered up and spat, her eyes so full of hate, you would've thought that woman was the devil himself."

The news enraged me. Poor Cathy, the soul of innocence, had cracked under the strain, suffered a psychotic break, and they still sent her off to get sliced up like a side of beef. A few hours after the operation, I called Stanford Hospital, introducing myself as "Doctor Gamel, Catherine Kohler's attending here at Valley Medical." God forbid they should know I was a lowly intern. "Stable"—that was the only word I could wheedle out of that stupid clerk.

A few days later, I got an afternoon off and drove up the Bay Shore Freeway, only to find Stanford Hospital a madhouse, with teams of interns and residents and medical students swarming every corridor. The first floor of the west wing was closed off for NBC to film a special on Shumway's heart-transplant team, so I had to take a freight elevator up to Ward West 3A. Cathy's bed was empty. Her roommate lay reading a magazine, rubbing a tassel of her soft brown hair against her lips.

She said, "Cathy's gone for a walk."

Cathy—walking! The words gave me a shock. Cathy lived in a bed, now and then in a wheelchair or on a gurney. I had never seen her walk. I wandered down the corridor, around the corner to Ward West 3B, across and back down West 3A. After two circuits I was about to reverse my direction, when—my God—there she was. I had passed without recognizing her.

She seemed so tall. Upright, ramrod straight, her head rising well above my shoulder—almost as tall as I was. And painfully rigid, her eyes showing the agony of every step. An IV pole bobbed beside her, dangling a bag of blood. The blood in the bag and in the IV line that passed beneath her collarbone looked dark, almost black. Beneath the terrycloth robe, her modest breasts showed perfect symmetry. The titanium rod had uncoiled her into a woman.

It couldn't be, but it was—Cathy. Yes, the green eyes, the hollow cheeks, the long nose a little broad at the tip, the neck and face pale against the pink robe, and yet…something had gone wrong. The trace of dusky suffocation had vanished. It was an ordinary face.

I spoke to her. "Yes. Fine. No," she said, answering my questions as reluctantly as ever, but now she looked me in the eye. A steady gaze, her face still impassive as a doll's. And ordinary. I couldn't get over that—such a pale, common face. Perhaps I missed the color, the indigo trace of asphyxia. Now her skin was dead white, palely translucent, like a polished wafer made from ivory or bone.

The loss of that trace carried a terrible meaning. She didn't need me. I was delighted, of course, absolutely delighted. About as happy, I would guess, as a mother whose precious child once lay in her arms but now stands six feet tall, with hair on his chest and a face full of pimples. Those who claim they never want to go back tell a dreadful lie. All precious things have their moment, and that moment is never—*never*—the last. The last moment is death.

Cathy's suffering would soon fade, the agony of each step healed by quick young tissues. Those green eyes had held no secrets meant only for me, no craving to be understood, no longing that could be served by innocent hands. She didn't want someone to stroke her brow or balm her soul. No, she wanted a surgeon—a man with a knife who could fix her body. Fitzy and I were eunuchs, useless wimps who had nursed her down a painful road to nowhere.

Cathy was not my patient. Soon she would be no one's patient. I had sought a new woman carved from the old flesh by a surgeon's knife, but in the majesty of her pain, I saw that she was lost to me forever. Cathy, Shoemaker, the doctors who sliced open her back—they got it right. I got it wrong. I had defended Cathy with all my heart, arguing against the cruel knife, yet in the end, my defeat had brought her triumph.

CHAPTER FIVE

A Quiet Departure

We were a distinguished group. At least we looked distinguished—five medical students in starched white jackets, alert and bright-eyed, sporting four beards and a ponytail. The ponytail was Mike Keane, a tall, spare figure with muttonchop sideburns. On special occasions he tied his straw-colored hair with a ribbon or a bone clip, but on weekday rounds he made do with a rubber band. My beard was red and curly, the bushiest of the four, since trimming exposed a mangy scattering of bare spots. My poker buddies had nicknamed me the Fat Man—the nickname of an obese character in *The Maltese Falcon* played by Sydney Greenstreet—and the beard gave my round face what I hoped was a professional mien.

We had been selected by James Goode, the chief resident at the Palo Alto VA Hospital, for his prestigious clinical tutorial. Under his watchful eye, we studied the science of medicine without getting bogged down in the details of day-to-day care. For us, standard textbooks were just the beginning. Day after day, we plumbed the esoteric depths by reading every journal we could get our hands on: *Monographs in Allergy*, *Recent Results in Cancer Research*, *Parasitology*, *The International Review of Thoracic Diseases*. Simon Rosenthal—the wunderkind of our group, a fidgety myope with a sleek beard and wire-rimmed glasses—earned a murmur of approval at morning rounds when he translated an abstract in *Acta Clinica Belgica* from the original Dutch.

Of course we had patients—the most fascinating cases in Northern California, gleaned from every wing of the hospital. They suffered from the rarest diseases, offered the most bizarre clinical presentations, and yielded lab values that ran off the chart. Doctor Goode, our cheerful, garrulous mentor, treated us with undeserved respect, but he also made certain we never touched a patient except under his cautious eye.

"Read the literature," he said. "You'll never get another chance like this."

Read we did. And write. Our write-ups on new patients spanned twenty, sometimes thirty pages, with a page or two of citations at the end. A daily progress note shorter than five pages was considered negligent. Our patients' charts soon bulged with nascent wisdom, but the most exciting chance to strut our stuff came during morning rounds. As we stood at each bedside, the student assigned to that patient waxed eloquent at great length, following the recently adopted formula known as SOAP:

Subjective—"Mr. Rackham complains of burning perirectal pain."

Objective—"My examination disclosed a hard, fixed, three-centimeter mass on his right buttock."

Assessment—"The endothelioma originating in his right kidney has metastasized to a lymph node in his buttock."

Plan—"We should increase his daily dose of methotrexate to twenty milligrams, as suggested by a recent study published in *The New England Journal of Medicine*."

For an ideal performance, the patient's chart was kept tightly closed, held against the presenter's chest to show that all this data had been committed to memory. Photocopies of relevant articles won extra points. When the student finished his spiel, his four colleagues offered their opinions. Then, ever so gently, Goode pointed out the errors: there are no lymph nodes in the buttocks; the lump was an abscess, not a metastasis; the patient's white count had dropped alarmingly, thus an increased dose of methotrexate would kill the poor man surely as a bullet. After rounds, shamed by the gaps in our knowledge, we rushed to the library to pore over yet more journals, while Goode wrote the orders and performed the tasks that kept our patients alive.

* * *

Our naïveté was immense. At that time, Stanford Medical School remained a naïve place, despite its worldwide reputation and a faculty that included four Nobel Prize winners. The problem had begun in 1959, seven years before my arrival, when an administrative genius decided to move the medical school from its original site in San

Francisco—where the indigent and unhealthy abounded, providing essential teaching material—to the trendy city of Palo Alto, the tofu capital of Northern California. Most of the faculty stayed in San Francisco, leaving the relocated school with few professors and almost no patients. The latter problem was soon but imperfectly remedied by recruiting patients with rare diseases from all over the world. Lupus, Hodgkin's disease, childhood cancers—the victims flooded into an elegant new hospital designed by Edward Durell Stone on a Spanish theme of open courtyards.

When I sent my mother a picture postcard showing the fountains at the entrance to Stanford Hospital, she thought it was my new apartment building. To my brief note, "Here's where I live," she responded, "How the hell can you afford a ritzy place like that?" Palm trees and hanging planters, together with the legendary sunshine of Northern California, gave a cheerful lift to some of the sickest patients on earth. But where were the indigent patients, with their common diseases and their dependence on student doctors for primary care?

Stanford had made a decision at the highest level: it would no longer encumber itself by training ordinary physicians. No, Stanford graduates would become the professors of the future, an elite cadre taught by the greatest scientific minds on earth. Arthur Kornburg and Joshua Lederberg, recent Nobel laureates, were recruited to chair the Biochemistry and Microbiology departments. During the next few years, two of their underlings also won Nobel Prizes. Research—publish or perish—became the catchword among the faculty.

From that time forth, no bedside grunt, no devotee of hands-on medicine, would ever earn tenure at Stanford. Instead, they appointed as the chairman of medicine a man who had published numerous papers but hadn't finished his formal training in internal medicine. Clinical rounds on some services began at five a.m., rousing patients from a sound sleep so the team could get an early start on the laboratory research that followed. Medical students were given blocks of free time to immerse themselves in petri dishes, cell cultures, and cages full of white mice. Generous grants from the National Institutes of Health allowed even the most junior faculty to hire these students as budding scientists. During freshman orientation, the dean assured us that Stanford would soon overtake Harvard as the vanguard of American medicine. No doubt Harvard's professors were quaking in their boots.

* * *

So there stood the five of us, bursting with information, eager to boost our egos by one-upping each other at every opportunity. We had read numerous textbooks and journals. We knew how to palpate the abdomen, percuss and auscultate the chest. Our learned ears could detect the splitting of the second heart sound into its two components, the opening snap of mitral stenosis, or the three components of a pericardial rub. No enlarged spleen or rock-hard liver could hide its secrets from our probing fingers. We knew our patients inside-out—vital signs, physical findings, laboratory reports. But alas, our minds harbored an unsuspected void.

And one sunny morning, there amidst our ignorance lay Nathan Newborn, an emaciated gentleman whose skin shone with a glossy tightness. Scleroderma, a rare disease, had transformed his skin into the color and consistency of polished mahogany. Carcinoid, an equally rare disease, seized his bowels with cramps and caused violent mood swings by releasing bursts of serotonin into his bloodstream. A nightmarish combination, for whatever agonies one illness spared him, the other was sure to cause. His only payoff was a monthlong stay at Stanford Hospital, where his two-disease combo had earned him the royal treatment. But now, his insurance long since exhausted, our team attended his wooden body while the diseases ran their dreadful course.

It was a fine Saturday morning. The hospital's east wing, an open ward with ten beds, had once served as a TB sanitarium. The California sun shone so bright through the tall windows it hurt our eyes. Since Doctor Goode had taken the morning off to attend his wife's third childbirth, our rounds would be supervised by Jerry Peggotty, a rheumatology fellow destined for a faculty appointment at Stanford.

None of us had met Doctor Peggotty. In all his years at Stanford, he had never set foot in the VA Hospital, and the first thing he did that morning was get lost. We had been waiting twenty minutes when a scruffy-looking fellow stormed up to the nursing station and—or so it seemed from a distance—got into an argument with the ward clerk. The two of them raised their voices and waved their arms, until at last the clerk pointed in our direction. The new arrival headed toward us with an impatient stride.

He was short and square and leaned a bit forward as he walked. Surely this was a doctor: his white coat suggested as much, but everything else—tennis shoes, faded jeans, an ill-knotted tie and wrinkled shirt—left the issue open to question. His long brown hair hung over his ears.

Peggotty introduced himself and then explained that he had been up all night doing a skin-graft experiment on salamanders. His hoarse voice suggested the final throes of exhaustion. His eyes were moist, almost glazed. Sleep dust matted his lashes. The man looked like he was on drugs, and the excitement had yet to begin.

The tableau of that sunlit ward remains vivid in my mind. The beds stood lined up in two rows along a waxed floor that shone like a mirror. At the bedside of the first patient, Mike Keane launched into his routine.

"Mister Oberon is a forty-seven-year-old white male with interstitial pneumonitis of unknown etiology. He entered our hospital six days ago complaining of...."

The first four patients went smoothly, though we were disappointed by Peggotty's lack of enthusiasm. How could he not gaze in wonder at such rare afflictions? When Mike handed him a reprint from *The International Journal of Autoimmune Diseases*, Peggotty read the title aloud—"A Survey of Interstitial Pneumonitis at Guy's Hospital"—then handed the article back to Mike. "Very interesting," he said. "Now, would someone please tell me about the next patient."

Nathan waited for us at the end of the row, his eyes half closed and his arms lying at his sides. Two nurses stood in the light of the tall windows, smiling and chatting as they changed his sheets—a tricky job when done with the patient lying motionless in the middle of the bed. Nathan seemed relaxed, unperturbed by their ministrations, even when they rolled his hard, smooth body from side to side to coax the clean sheet beneath him. His dusky face, a contrast to the plaid pajamas he wore that day, was peaceful as a mummy's. His chest was also still except for a gasping breath every few seconds. I remember thinking how fortunate it was that the bouts of agitation brought on by his carcinoid disease had finally abated.

"Oh, please go right ahead," said one of the nurses, smiling at the circle of doctors gathered around the bed. "We're almost through."

As soon as the nurses had bundled up the dirty sheets and moved on to the next bed, Simon Rosenthal, Nathan's assigned student, clutched the chart to his chest and launched into his presentation.

"Mr. Nathan Newborn is a sixty-four-year-old Afro-American male who suffers from scleroderma and carcinoid. His case was reported in the March 1969 issue of *Recent Results in Cancer Research*. During the six weeks Mr. Newborn has been on our service...."

Simon was good. Very good. His voice had gravitas, with a care and cadence to his diction that said, "I'm one hell of a smart guy." He always wore a freshly ironed white coat. I envied his thick, sleek beard, but what bothered me most was an encyclopedic memory that made me sound like a moron. He had only one defect, a tiny flaw: his nails were bitten to the quick. For days I had watched him out the corner of my eye—on rounds, in the cafeteria, in the library—but never saw his fingers come near his mouth. A secret vice, like masturbation. The thought lifted my spirits. And there was the wonderful morning when Simon had shown up for rounds with a brown shoe on one foot and a black shoe on the other. The rest of us laughed raucously, rocking back and forth and slapping our thighs, the pleasure of the moment enhanced by the dark, sullen blush ascending from Simon's collar to the roots of his jet-black hair.

As we stood in the sunshine—gathered around Nathan's bed, gazing at his peaceful face—Simon's voice gave a soothing *basso continuo* to the debacle that would soon unfold. Nathan lay still, his arms at his sides atop the fresh sheets.

"Mr. Newborn's last urine analysis showed four-plus white cells and a trace of hematuria, so we're working him up for a urinary tract infection but so far…"

"Wait!"

It was Peggotty, our temporary attending. His explosive shout filled the ward. Everyone stared at him. The man had gone mad. His jaw hung open and his eyes, staring at Nathan, seemed to bulge out of his head. The silence that followed his outburst was broken by a rattling gasp from Nathan's throat.

"My God," Peggotty said, "what…what's going on here?" He staggered toward Nathan's bed, then turned to look wildly about at the circle of puzzled faces. We squirmed with embarrassment and looked down at our feet. The man was having a psychotic break, perhaps from an overdose of a recreational drug. Amphetamine? Mescaline? LSD? There was a lot of that going around the San Francisco Bay Area, especially among physicians.

"Tell me," he said, "this patient…is he…is he a no code?" As Peggotty spoke, a rising note of panic in his voice, he lurched forward and pressed his fingers against Nathan's stringy neck. We stood dumbstruck. What in the world was he doing? I tried to decide how we could help Peggotty through his crisis.

"My God!" he shouted at last, snatching open Nathan's pajama top so abruptly the buttons flew off, exposing his sallow, bony chest. Not until he pounded on that chest and forced air into Nathan's gaping mouth with his own lips did the five of us suspect the truth.

The clerk rushed across the ward to pull Peggotty away so the poor man could die in peace. Nathan was indeed a no code.

* * *

Peggotty glared at us as though we were a pack of idiots. We stood silent, abashed, wincing like children whose hands had been smacked by a ruler. Of course, Nathan's last gasps were Cheyne-Stokes respirations— the unmistakable mark of a patient's final agony. We had studied textbooks, we knew the facts, but no one connected the facts on a printed page with death in the flesh. Death was our blind spot.

Along with the nurses who tucked clean sheets under Nathan's expiring body, we had been misled. There was the sunshine, the blue sky, the light-filled windows—a conspiracy of ambience. Who but a battle-scarred veteran, a real doctor, could imagine that death might visit on a day as fresh and bright as life itself?

CHAPTER SIX

The Golden Boy

During my fourth year of medical school, I took a clerkship on Ward East 1A, Stanford's notorious medical ward. Most of the patients were desperately ill, suffering from rare and often incurable diseases. Black humor, whispered only in private, suggested a sign that should be placed over the ward's entrance: *SURRENDER ALL HOPE, YE WHO ENTER HERE.*

East 1A was devoted to exotic diseases, diseases so rare and difficult that doctors throughout the world gladly referred them to us. As a result of this policy, I saw many cases of lupus erythematosus, Hodgkin's disease, and hairy cell leukemia but not a single case of pneumococcal pneumonia. Indeed, many of my patients had pneumonia, but this was because chemotherapy had destroyed their immunity, and their lungs were infected by a bacterium whose name I had never heard. My one heart attack victim was not an overweight smoker with atherosclerosis but a teenaged Inuit referred from Alaska with lupus arteritis.

The senior resident on East 1A was James Goode, the same physician who had taught my clinical tutorial at the VA hospital. Prior to his residency, Goode had served as the medical officer on a nuclear submarine. A year spent patrolling beneath the icy waters of the North Atlantic gave him the poise he would need to deal with Jason M., our new intern. A wunderkind with brown eyes, dark hair, and a warm, impish smile, Jason had already earned the nickname Golden Boy by publishing an astounding number of scientific articles.

Those who quaked at the thought of being cared for by medical students could have rested assured: nowhere in North America was a medical student allowed to touch a patient or write an order without authorization from a licensed physician. Thus on East 1A, I wrote orders in my patients' charts, but the nurses would do nothing until Goode had countersigned them. Interns like Jason were a different matter. As licensed physicians, their orders required no prior authorization. And thereupon hangs a tale.

During morning rounds, he gave brilliant presentations, reeling off minutiae gleaned from journals and from his patients' charts. When he finished his spiel, Goode would say, "Great job, Doctor M. Now, what do you suggest we do for this patient?"

Jason never hesitated.

"I think we should cut back his Immuran by ten milligrams and add potassium to his IV, about twenty milliequivalents per hour. And we should keep an eye on his temperature, get blood cultures if it spikes over 100. In the latest issue of *The American Journal of Oncology*, a group at Harvard reported that 53 percent of their patients with small-cell lymphoma developed septicemia at some time during their first admission."

Jason knew his stuff, no doubt about that, but he was a by-the-book doctor. When Mrs. Gorman, a large patient with systemic lupus, insisted on taking her daily bottle of Fletcher's Castoria, an over-the-counter laxative, Jason consulted the *Hopkins Intern's Handbook* he always carried in his jacket pocket. Under the heading *Laxatives*, he found only the injunction, "Routine laxatives serve no useful purpose and should be avoided."

So much for Mrs. Gorman's request. Jason wrote in her chart, "Under no circumstances is this patient to receive a laxative of any sort," and the nurses followed his order. At rounds the next morning, Mrs. Gorman pleaded, "Oh, Doctor M., I've drunk a bottle of Fletcher's Castoria every day for ten years. If I don't take it, my bowels will seize up."

The woman was a prophet, but Jason didn't get the message.

"Forget it," he said. "You don't need the stuff, and I'm not going to give it to you."

Things continued thus until the morning Mrs. Gorman sobbed, "My God, Doctor M., I'm so bloated I can hardly breathe. I haven't had a bowel movement since I came to the hospital."

Jason froze in his tracks and stood gazing into space. I could see the wheels turning behind those startled brown eyes: *Hmmm...she was admitted on Wednesday...this is Thursday week...yikes—eight days!*

The poor woman's bowels, absent their explosive daily dose of Fletcher's Castoria, had shut down like a locked safe. Jason grabbed his *Hopkins Intern's Handbook* and read, "Obstipation: Severe and obstinate constipation due to a variety of causes. May lead to fecal impaction and intestinal obstruction."

"Oh no!" Jason said. He rushed to the nursing station, sat down, and bit his nails. He was in trouble. So was Mrs. Gorman. I suggested we wait until Doctor Goode returned and seek his advice, but Jason would hear nothing of it. A Golden Boy never screws up—at least, he never gets caught screwing up. Jason would handle this problem before word of his idiocy got back to Goode. Things seemed to take a turn for the better when a nurse overheard our discussion and offered advice.

"Try a milk and molasses enema," she said. "It works every time."

"Really?" Jason said. The thought had never occurred to him. "OK, hurry up, let's get going."

Within minutes, a quart of equal parts milk and molasses had been stirred together, poured in an enema bag, and infused into Mrs. Gorman's rectum. We told her to hold it in as long as she could, then parked her on the toilet in her private bathroom to await deliverance. Jason remained upbeat until a disturbing groan from Mrs. Gorman's room made it clear our adventure wasn't over. Deep within our memories, there lurked enough knowledge to predict the impending disaster, but neither of us had put together the two crucial pieces of the puzzle.

Piece number one: a bottle of Fletcher's Castoria, when poured down the gullet every day for years on end, knocks the colon into a coma, a state of atonic paralysis just this side of death. The bowel movement that a copious enema would induce in a normal person was not part of Mrs. Gorman's immediate future. Rather, our quart of milk and molasses lay stalled, pooled, motionless, trapped in a colon flaccid as the bladder of a dead pig.

Piece number two: molasses has a strong tendency to pull water from the delicate membranes lining the colon. Thus what had begun as a one-quart enema was well on its way to becoming a two-quart enema, and in the fullness of time would become a one-gallon enema, perhaps more. Though neither Jason nor I could calculate the precise volume gathering in the poor woman's bowels, the rising pitch of her groans left no doubt things were getting worse by the moment. Something had to be done.

Just as Mrs. Gorman wailed, "Oh my God, Doctor! I swear I can't take it another minute," James Goode rushed into the room.

"Hey, guys," he said. "What's going on?"

Jason and I sat by Mrs. Gorman's bathroom with our hands in our laps. We knew our concoction had ballooned her colon to the size of a football, but when it came to remedies, our brains remained perfect vacuums. Jason, blushing and stammering, confessed his sins. Goode gave a weary sigh.

"OK, Jason," he said, "let's get her to the sigmo room."

* * *

Modern technology has stolen from medicine some of its most exciting moments. For example, doctors and patients no longer share the delights of the classic sigmoidoscope, a rigid, chrome-plated instrument the size and shape of an automobile exhaust pipe. Instead, doctors now opt for a sissified gadget, flexible as a strand of cooked spaghetti and not much thicker than a pencil. But Mrs. Gorman's crisis occurred forty years ago. For her, there was no escape.

When she crouched knees-to-chest on the sigmo table, her naked rear loomed large. Doctor Goode inserted the chrome pipe, but as the instrument inched its way into the patient's rectum, he made an unpleasant discovery: if he continued his search for the pocket of fluid lurking deep in her colon, the need to keep his right eye near the lens of the sigmo would soon force him to tuck his ears between her enormous buttocks. A few millimeters before contact, he backed away, gave Jason a malignant smile, and beckoned for him to take the scope. Later, in the privacy of the drug room, James explained his logic.

"Dammit, Jason, it was only fair. You started this mess."

When the mini-Vesuvius finally erupted, spraying milk and molasses and bodily fluids in a wide arc, Goode and I cowered in the far corners of the sigmo room. Jason had to shower and change into fresh scrubs. During the ordeal, I chortled to myself, delighted that the Golden Boy had made a first-class fool of himself.

My time would come.

* * *

Since the 1960s, Stanford has sent its residents to Valley Medical Center so they can experience life in the real world, away from the medical arcana of Ward East 1A. Thanks to this arrangement, my month as an intern on the medicine service at Valley Medical Center proved more challenging than I had expected. My resident was Walter O'Connor, a superb physician, but he took call only every sixth night. Interns took call every third night, and thus, on Walter's nights off, I worked with a resident from another team. This turned out to be none other than Jason M., the Golden Boy himself, now a first-year Stanford resident serving his time at Valley Medical Center.

Poor Jason. Away from the hallowed halls of Stanford, he suffered a nervous collapse. At Valley Medical Center, patients poured in by the dozens, suffering from every disease in the book—diabetes, hypertension, emphysema, congestive failure, myocardial infarction—while Jason's expertise included only a few exotic ailments. His most trying moments came in the dark of night, when he was summoned down to the ER.

During a typical night, the resident on call would examine between one- and two-dozen ER patients. Of these, a poised, confident physician admitted only a fraction, perhaps four or five. For the remainder, the resident would devise a treatment plan and send them home. This challenge called for good judgment. It was considered poor form to send a patient home only to have them drop dead a few hours later.

I confronted this dilemma myself when I served as an intern in the ER. Patients often had multiple diseases, any one of which might kill them within the next day or two. Even if I could calculate the probability of death from each disease—which no doctor could, except in the crudest terms—the question remained: at what threshold could I risk sending the patient home? A one-in-ten chance they would die? One in a hundred? One in a thousand?

Indeed, the ER was a crapshoot, but as an intern I could always lean on my resident. If I asked for too many consults, he might give me a bad report at the end of the rotation. I could live with that. The resident bore the burden of the final decision: admit the patient or bite the bullet and send her home.

These decisions drove Jason into a frenzy. He flipped through the chart a dozen times, rushed back again and again to reexamine the patient, shouted at the ER clerk if she couldn't find every scrap of the patient's old records, all the while biting his nails and pulling his hair. He paced the floor. He ordered more tests, backlogging the ER until gurneys filled the hallway and the cast room. Finally, after hours of agonizing indecision, he admitted almost every patient. The Golden Boy could not tolerate uncertainty. Since half of these admissions came to my team, the morning after one of Jason's orgies gave Walter and me a good laugh. As I sat at the ward counter working my way through a stack of charts, my resident strode onto the ward, thumped the stack, and laughed.

"OK, Gamel," he said with a sardonic smile, "what kind of crap did Jason dump on us this time?"

One by one, Walter examined our new patients, reviewed their charts, and then—in almost every case— sent them home. One patient stands out in my mind as an exemplar of Jason's indecision. She was immensely obese, took eight medications, and complained of shortness of breath, abdominal pains, and swollen ankles.

The morning after Jason admitted her to our service, Walter grabbed the chest X-ray taken the night before and slapped it in the view box. It was useless, the details of the heart and lungs obscured by adipose tissue. He slapped in an old film taken five years before. There had been no change.

Walter looked at the EKG done the night before. It was useless, the voltage so diminished by adipose tissue that the tracing showed only tiny, indecipherable blips. He pulled out an old EKG done years before. No change.

Walter examined the patient. Her breath and heart sounds were inaudible. When he probed her abdomen, there were no palpable masses, no guarding or rigidity. He asked whether any of her symptoms were getting better.

"Oh, no, Doctor," she said. "My breathing, my stomach, my ankles, everything is still bad, just as bad as they've been for years and years."

Walter refilled her prescriptions and sent her home. It took all morning to discharge the rest of Jason's admissions. When at last we sat down to lunch in the hospital cafeteria, Jason caught sight of us and rushed to our table.

"Hey, what did you guys do with that huge lady, the one with those terrible lungs? And her ankles, my God they were massive. She must have had two inches of pitting edema."

"Well, Jason," Walter said, "we sent her home."

"Oh no! How the hell could you do that?"

"It's OK, Jason. We beefed up her Lasix prescription. She'll be fine."

"And what about the guy with that awful chest pain?"

"He had acid indigestion. We gave him a bottle of Tums and sent him home."

"Oh no! How the hell could you do that?"

And so it went. When Jason finished his year at Valley Medical Center, he could boast a perfect record: not one of the infinitesimally few patients he sent home from the ER died within the next twenty-four hours. I doubt that any other resident at Valley Medical Center could make that claim.

* * *

Five years after my internship, I was invited to give a talk at a famous research institute in Washington, D.C. Jason, now a high-ranking member of the institute's faculty, served as my host. He gave me a warm greeting. While introducing me to the audience, he touted my scientific achievements, though they were a mere flyspeck compared to his. Afterward, over lunch, Jason and I reminisced about our years together at Stanford. He was enthusiastic, full of the joys, his dark eyes shining as he spoke of his plans for the future. And indeed, it all came to pass. During the next thirty years, Jason published 300 papers. His research led to new treatments for a variety of devastating diseases. Indeed, he ranks among the most accomplished scientists of his era. I wouldn't be surprised to see him win a Nobel Prize.

It was a privilege to know the man. An obsessive-compulsive workaholic, a stubborn but sweet-tempered polymath, he suffered from a paralyzing excess of compassion. When confronted by the issues of life and death on a global scale, he charged ahead, the bravest and most talented of men. But when Jason laid his hands on patients and looked them in the eye, the faintest chance he might cause harm drove him berserk. A strange fellow indeed—a tormented physician who fled bedside medicine to save thousands of lives as a research scientist. His flight also saved thousands of patients from a needless hospital admission. Like all wise physicians, Jason healed himself.

Would that the world had more like him.

CHAPTER SEVEN

The Pluperfect Fraud

S anta Clara County Hospital was built in 1836 to care for the indigents of San Jose, California. It served this function until the 1960s, when the board of directors decided to lure paying patients through their doors. They changed the name to Santa Clara Valley Medical Center and then forged an affiliation with Stanford Hospital, but their efforts achieved only modest success. It was a matter of status. The aristocrats of Northern California still referred to Valley Medical Center as the county hospital. They considered its doctors all hapless students, and they wanted nothing to do with the riff-raff that crowded its charity wards.

This snobbery stole from me a patient who became a landmark in my career when I diagnosed his disease at twenty paces. Late one night, halfway through my ER shift, I watched a nurse lead Mark Cisko to a gurney. A student at nearby San Jose City College, he was thin, of average height, and had short, dark hair. His flushed face suggested a fever. A grimace contorted his mouth every time he lifted his right foot to take a step.

A voice in my head said, *I'll bet that kid has appendicitis.* The moment he lay on a gurney, I introduced myself, explained what I was about to do, then pulled up his shirt and gently pressed my fingertips into the right lower quadrant of his abdomen. He screamed in pain. An ER nurse measured his temperature at 103. Half an hour later, when his blood test confirmed a high white count, I started an IV and paged Sam Watanabe, the surgery resident on call that night. Sam was 6'2" tall, the tallest Japanese man I have ever met. He examined Marcus and glanced through his chart.

"Good job, Gamel," he said. "It's been a slow night. Talk to the family, and we'll get him up to the OR when ortho finishes their case. It shouldn't be more than an hour."

So there lay my patient, his lab work done and his IV in place, scheduled for surgery within the hour by a fine pair of hands. The OR nurses all agreed—Sam's appendectomies were the best, a work of art from first cut to last stitch. But it was not to be. My phone call woke up Mark's mother in Los Altos Hills. As soon as she understood what was happening, she spewed a string of invectives, warning that if any so-called doctor at that goddamn county hellhole laid a knife on her son, she'd sue our pants off.

An hour later, the battle-axe proved as good as her word when she stormed into the ER, a scrawny, enraged woman in a black leotard. A rope of dark hair swung down her back. Judging by the tantrum she threw, one might have thought we were about to mutilate her son rather than save his life. Poor Mark. Feverish, writhing in pain, he groaned as attendants loaded him onto an ambulance that would bear him off to a private hospital fifty miles away. The mother's snobbery would delay his operation for hours. I never found out how it went, but I imagined his surgeon to be a doddering old coot with an office in Los Altos Hills, the scalpel trembling in his hand while he tried to remember whether to make the incision on the right or the left side of the abdomen.

* * *

Despite scenes like this, Valley Medical Center held its own with the landed gentry. Every ambulance driver in the county knew where to take the victims of wrecks, knifings, and gunshots. Most of these patients had no insurance, but now and then a rich burgher with a crushed chest or a bullet through his abdomen would end up at Valley Medical Center. However fat his wallet, a man with blood pouring through an open wound was damn glad to see two or three of our doctors rush to his side the moment his gurney rolled into the ER.

We also had our share of nontrauma patients. True, private hospitals offered posh lobbies, catered meals, and a battalion of well-paid nurses, but at night, all their doctors went home. Thus the truly sick, no matter how much they paid for medical insurance, often found themselves trundled off to our humble wards, where round-the-clock doctoring came at no extra charge. It was always a treat to admit a member of the upper crust. The family—frightened by their loved one's illness and even more frightened when the illness took a turn for the worse—looked on in wonder as attendants wheeled the patient into a room at the disparaged Valley Medical Center. Moments later, when an intern young enough to be their grandson came to examine the patient, some family members were ready for the smelling salts.

Yet we always won them over. We were always there. One night out of three, the interns worked a thirty-six-hour shift, roaming the wards until the early hours of the morning. On the other two nights, they would go home somewhere between eight p.m. and midnight, but only after introducing their patients to the colleague who was on call that evening. This beat the hell out of the coverage provided by private doctors, busy fellows who stopped in for a five-minute visit once a day, then drove miles down the freeway to their offices or homes. At three in the morning, when a patient's heart went into ventricular tachycardia and his blood pressure dropped to 60/30, an intern at the bedside was worth more than a dozen specialists lying at home asleep. Around the clock, seven days a week, the families huddled outside the ICU saw our doctors rush again and again to the bedside of desperate patients. And when a page operator announced, "Code blue in room 23," half a dozen residents crowded into that room before a minute had elapsed.

Most of these doctors were training for a medical or surgical specialty, but the chain of command was carefully supervised. An intern fresh out of medical school, I was seldom more than fifty feet away from a junior resident who knew twice more than I did, while he or she answered in turn to a third- or fourth-year resident. At the top of the pyramid stood the attending physicians, board-certified faculty members with decades of experience. They conducted rounds every day and staffed all of the major surgeries.

Irony of ironies, that disparaged hospital delivered the best medical care in the county. I would not have hesitated to admit a loved one to the Valley Medical Center.

* * *

Despite this well-ordered arrangement, one experience plumbed the depths of my incompetence. At first, the west nursery seemed idyllic: all the patients were healthy newborns waiting out their three-day stay in the hospital. If a woman delivered a preemie or an infant fell ill, the unfortunate child was rushed down the hall to the east nursery, where most of the patients were preemies on respirators, with two interns and two residents working around the clock to keep them alive.

The west nursery also featured Mrs. Kanamoto, the only nurse on the ward. The living embodiment of a Swiss watch, she was tiny and elegant, with dark eyes and jet-black hair. Her grooming was immaculate, her face bright and cheerful. Mrs. K., as we called her, had superb management skills. She kept the rooms spotless. In the supply cabinets, the items sat lined up in perfect rows. With little sign of effort, she saw to it that every day in the west nursery ran a smooth and peaceful course.

As Mrs. K. introduced me to my new patients, I thought myself the luckiest intern at Valley Medical. In the main room, where twenty diaper-swaddled newborns lay in bassinets, a large window allowed relatives to view their beloved cherubs. Since the room was kept at a constant 80 degrees, I took off my white coat and worked in my scrub shirt.

"Doctor Gamel," Mrs. K. said, "your job is to examine each new baby when the OB intern brings it over from the delivery room. After that, you must visit them every day to make sure they're healthy and feeding well."

I felt a twinge of anxiety.

"Ah...about this feeding business," I said. "And the diapers...er...who..."

"Oh, Doctor Gamel, no need to worry," she said with a reassuring smile. "We have lots of volunteers and nurses' aides. You're the doctor; you must do only the important things."

Whew—that was close! Some years before, when my sister had delivered her first child, the bald, wrinkled, red-faced creature looked so hideous I couldn't stand to go near it. The smell of a loaded diaper and the sight of its contents made me sick. There were no other births in my immediate family, and during my pediatric rotation in medical school, I had cared for no infants. Thanks to these privations, my heart carried a dark secret: never in my life had I fed a baby or changed its diaper. And yet, as I looked around at the chubby cheeks and button noses of my new patients, a glow of affection warmed my heart. Thanks to Mrs. K. and her minions, I could remain aloof, a benign monarch peering down on his helpless, needy subjects.

True, I had to examine the little rascals the moment they arrived, still damp from the bath that had washed away the amniotic fluid, but newborn exams are a snap: look in the eyes, ears, nose, and throat; listen to the tiny chest; press my fingers against the sweet little belly; and check out the genitals and the anus. Oh, and count the fingers and toes. Voila! Finis! If I discovered a cleft palate or an imperforate anus, I would trot the child over to the east nursery and hand it off to my exhausted colleagues.

My first day on the job, I made an astonishing discovery: these tiny bags of protoplasm had people inside them. One would be full of fire, thrashing about until a spindly arm caught the tubing of my stethoscope and snatched it from around my neck. Another would lie motionless in the bassinet, her eyes squeezed tight, her balled fists pressed beneath her chin. One would have a mat of jet-black hair atop a chubby face, while another would be a bald and browless creature with sunken cheeks. Some babies would rest in my arms like sleeping kittens, and still others would squirm and squall the moment I touched them. During midnight rounds, I surveyed my kingdom, a room filled with life in the making.

The west nursery proved a wonderful awakening, but disaster lurked even there, among the most innocent souls on earth. My first morning on the job, I noticed that several mothers—an eclectic mix of Caucasians, Hispanics, and African-Americans—had gathered in a small room adjoining the nursery. Many looked older than I was. Some had other children with them big enough to walk and talk and dress themselves. One by one, Mrs. K. carried out the new infants and gave them to the mothers. Ah, I realized at last, these were the three-day-olds, ready to go home. But why didn't the mothers take their babies and head for the discharge desk?

"Oh, Mrs. K.," I said. "What are those mothers waiting for?"

"Ah, Doctor Gamel, they're waiting for you."

"Waiting for me!" My pulse shot up. I didn't like the sound of that. "Why are they waiting for me?"

"Doctor, you must give them instructions."

"Instructions? What instructions?"

"They need to know the little things, like how to bathe the baby, when and how much to feed it, and what to do when the baby wakes up in the night. And they want any tips you might have for changing the diapers. Mothers are always afraid they might injure their baby with the pins."

I stood silent, frozen, staring at Mrs. K. I stared for a long time, searching for the trace of a smile, for some assurance this was a joke. No dice. Her doll-like face remained smooth and stern. But I had to escape. Surely she would relent when I dropped my bomb: at twenty-eight years of age, I had yet to poke a nipple into a baby's mouth or wipe its bottom. My confession didn't work. She held her ground.

"You're a doctor," she said, meeting my panicked eyes with a hard, steady gaze. "Your patients expect you to know these things."

"But, Mrs. K., don't you have any children?" I asked, grasping at one last, desperate hope.

"Oh, yes." Her face brightened. "A little three-year-old girl. If you'd like, I will show you a picture."

"Good! Perfect!" I said. "See, you're a nurse, you've taken care of babies for years and years, and you have a baby of your own. You're the perfect person to talk to these mothers."

"Oh, no." Her smile vanished. "That won't do—they don't want a nurse. They want knowledge from a doctor, so they will know they can trust what you tell them."

Four decades later, that last sentence—which I recall with exquisite clarity—strikes me as the funniest thing I've ever heard, but at the time I was too terrified to see the humor. Logic had failed. My only hope was to turn on the charm.

Over the course of my life, I have begged many women. I have begged for love, I have begged for money, and yes, I have begged for sex. But all those efforts seem mere trifles—paltry, half-hearted requests, hardly worth the effort—when compared to the show I put on for Mrs. K. I was by no means a handsome man, but I was young, vigorous, and skilled at the persuasive arts that had served me so well with my mother, sister, and girlfriends.

No dice. My pleas fell to the ground like spent arrows. Mrs. K.— rail thin, five feet tall, the face of a China doll—stood solid as a rock.

I stood on a plank, an ocean below, a saber goading my back.

* * *

A few years after this humiliation, I distinguished myself by walking into a delicatessen wearing only a T-shirt and boxer shorts. It was all quite reasonable. When I met a friend at a men's club in San Mateo to play a few games of squash, there were no tennis shorts in my gym bag. Since the club didn't allow women on the premises, I slipped my boxers on over my jock strap and headed or the court. After the games, I threw down the racquet, mopped the sweat off my face, grabbed my wallet, and rushed to the deli next door for a quart of soda water. Most of the time, the place was all but empty, but on that day it seemed like a full tour bus had just disgorged its passengers. While waiting in a long line to pay for the soda, I became aware of two sensations: I felt more air circulating about my nether parts than was usual for a man standing in a public place, and others in the line seemed to be casting sidelong glances in my direction.

A lucky man would have worn a pair of plain white boxers on that fateful day, leaving bystanders uncertain whether they were tennis shorts. Not me. My underdrawers were unequivocal, adorned front and back with paisley gewgaws. I fought an urge to rush from the store, but that would have encouraged my audience to collapse in peals of helpless laughter. Instead, my face aflame, I shifted from foot to foot for what seemed like an hour, paid for the soda water, and then strolled back to the club at the leisurely pace of a man with all the time in the world.

I mention this episode because it proved the second-most-humiliating moment of my life, measuring only seven on a scale of one-to-ten. My west nursery debasement measured ten and a half. There is perhaps a man on earth who felt himself a more ridiculous fool than I did as I spoke to those mothers. There is perhaps a man who choked more painfully on his words when he told them how to change their infants' diapers and mix their formula. There is perhaps a man whose face turned a brighter shade of red or who came closer to fleeing the room with his coattails flying, but I doubt it.

So great was my panic, I would have collapsed had Mrs. K. not handed me a crib sheet at the last moment. There, in clear bold letters, she had written:

Diapers   Check for moisture or odor every hour or
                   when baby cries
               Clean bottom with moist tissues
               Dry and powder every time
               Keep pins pointed away from baby's skin

Formula   Heat in pot filled with water
               Test temperature by sprinkling a few
                   drops on your wrist
                      ...

* * *

My first wife was a cool, aloof woman, given to subtle humor and quiet laughter, but when I told her the west nursery story, she lost it.

"You!" she shouted, clapping her hands and rocking back and forth in her chair. "You—telling mothers how to take care of their babies!"

She laughed off and on all evening, laughed until tears streamed down her cheeks, then woke me several times in the night. Her performance gave me an idea. The next day, as Mrs. K. shepherded me toward the waiting room for my second-morning debacle, I made one last attempt at escape. Logic hadn't worked, so it was time for a little humor.

"Mrs. K.," I said, "if you make me do this again, God will laugh so hard, she might fall off her throne."

"Ha ha ha," she said. "Oh, Doctor Gamel, you very clever."

No smile. No dice.

I settled into my chair. The mothers fell silent and pulled their chairs into a semicircle. Some gathered their older children around them. I heard one whisper, "You shush up—this here's the doctor." I gazed around at the pleasant, trusting faces of women who had nursed two or three infants and changed a thousand diapers.

"Now," I said, "I know many of you worry about how to manage your child's diapers. You don't want him to lie around for hours in a dirty diaper, but then you don't want to drive yourself crazy fussing over him all the time. And I know you worry about sticking the baby with a pin. Here's what I suggest...."

* * *

Fifteen years later, when my son Richard was a few days old, I changed my first diaper. Two years after that, I was invited to Chicago to give a talk on ocular cancers. It was the annual meeting of the American Academy of Ophthalmology, and thousands of physicians and scientists filled an amphitheater the size of a ballpark. An hour before my talk, while sorting through my slides in an alcove beneath the amphitheater, I noticed that the man sitting next to me seemed in bad shape. Sweat beaded his forehead. His hands trembled as he sorted his slides. When he glanced over at me, I responded with a sympathetic smile.

"Oh, my God," he said, "I hate this stuff. I've never given a talk before, and the thought of all those people watching makes me nervous as hell. I couldn't sleep a wink last night. How about you?"

"Oh, no," I said. "This stuff doesn't bother me at all."

I wanted to explain how Mrs. K. had cured forever my fear of public speaking, but the poor man would not have understood. You had to be there.

CHAPTER EIGHT

Pendulous Love

"Mrs. Badenhaus wasn't admitted to my service!"
That's what I told my wife—shouted it,
really—the moment I walked through the
door. She was reading a book. She was always reading
and hated to be disturbed, but this time, aroused by my
fervor, she marked her place with a finger and looked
up. Quiet. Attentive. Impatient. In the end I gave up on
sharing the news.

"Oh, nothing," I said. "Forget it."

It was not the sort of thing that interested her, but it
would prove the most spectacular stroke of luck during
the year of my internship. If Mrs. Badenhaus had been
admitted a few minutes earlier, Valley Medical Center's
all-time disaster would have fallen upon my shoulders,
adding to a list of tribulations that included two obstructed
gallbladders, a perirectal abscess the size of a hen's egg, a
grandmother in florid delirium tremens, and a half-dozen

GI hemorrhages, two of them so deep in hepatic coma they had to be diapered.

A month before, I had won the Chivas Regal Award for admitting the most jaundiced patient in the hospital. My champion was a Russian émigré whose iron will survived Stalin's reign of terror, but his flesh-and-blood liver floated away on a river of vodka. His comatose face had swollen lips, half-closed eyes, the porous sheen of a ripe lemon. Drool from the corner of his mouth stained his pillowcase with yellow blots. His breath smelled like urine—a condition due in part to bad genes: three of his four brothers had preceded him, each (according to my patient's wife) lying in his coffin more jaundiced than the last. The wife had a hot temper and puffy cheeks filigreed with purple veins. At ten o'clock in the morning, she reeked of liquor. A few hours before her husband's death, an attack of tremors sent her scurrying to Mellow Dee's.

That night I gazed at my own wife as she lay reading under the glow of our bedroom lamp. I tried to concentrate on *Harrison's Textbook of Medicine*, but I couldn't take my eyes off her beautiful, sober face.

* * *

Mrs. Badenhaus brought a refreshing change to a hospital awash in jaundice and hemorrhage. She drank her share—two six-packs a day, by her husband's account—but her liver was fine, a tolerance the GI consultant attributed to adequate nutrition, though "adequate" was hardly an adequate term for Mrs. Badenhaus. She weighed 430 pounds. To accommodate her bulk, an orderly wired two beds together with bent coat hangers. The visual spectacle stopped me in my tracks: one head—a large head, perfectly round—sat atop a mountainous body that seemed to call for two or three. She had huge nostrils, a dreamy morphine smile, deep-set eyes with a Mongolian slant. Her pasty arms were as big as thighs and damp with sweat.

Mrs. Badenhaus suffered an unclean disease. On the apron of fat that hung down to her knees, an ulcer had melted through the skin, gouging a crater the size of a dishpan. Pus from the wound teemed with staph, strep, pseudomonas, E. coli—every bacterium in the book. During dressing changes, the odor crept over *C* ward, fouling the air like toxic gas. Treatment was a challenge. Antibiotics might work, but a tremendous body demands a tremendous dose, and fat has poor circulation, especially infected fat. The blue team's only hope was to drip $600 worth of gentamycin into her veins every day.

Yes, Mrs. Badenhaus was admitted to *C* ward by the blue team. My service, the red team, shared the same ward, so I saw Big Momma, as she was called, on morning and evening rounds, but I didn't have to change her pus-soaked dressings or write two pages of orders in her chart every day. The blue team sent out a desperate call for help. Specialty services swarmed around her bed—GI, dermatology, rehab, infectious disease, plastic surgery—all scratching their heads, wringing their hands, making vague suggestions ("Enhance circulation... stimulate revascularization...increase antibiotic penetration...") for a cure that would go down in the annals of Valley Medical Center as the case of the year. Yet in the end it wasn't the medical challenge but passion, a love triangle of sorts, that kept tongues wagging all over the hospital. The *C* ward charge nurse fell in love with Mrs. Badenhaus' husband.

* * *

Johnnie was an attractive older woman, a little past forty, with a willowy figure, an angular face, and long, dark hair—suspiciously dark for her age. I liked Johnnie, liked her more and more as the days and nights wore on. It was my fate to fall at least a little in love with every woman who resembled my wife, a skinny dark-haired creature who had inherited the full, sensual lips of her father. Since adolescence, I have felt a surge of lust for thin women whose subdued smile promises a chilly aloofness from the human race that might give way to the one special person—me—among all the souls on earth. My wife was the chilliest, the most aloof, the most beautiful of them all. I loved her dearly, yet after five years of marriage, the icy detachment that bound me like a slave had left me desperate and as lonely as a castaway.

So yes, I was married but drawn to Johnnie because she resembled my wife. When I first arrived on *C* ward, Johnnie was skittish, avoided eye contact, and kept to herself for a week, but early one morning, over the corpse of a failed resuscitation, all that vanished. My back throbbed. My legs trembled. Exhaustion and failure had brought me to the verge of tears, yet at that moment, Johnnie looked at me with a gaze so steady it held my body up against the aching force of gravity, then covered my hand with hers as it rested on the pale, hairless chest of the dead patient. Her eyes said, *Give it up, John. You've done all you could do*. There was warmth in her touch, a tender pressure that lifted my spirits. Here was a loving and lovely woman—but a nurse, a colleague, too risky for romantic entanglement. Just what I needed. My nerves couldn't endure the turmoil of an affair, the risks of carnal penetration, but the tenderness of Johnnie's touch sent a thrill into my barren life.

We both knew well the rules that governed our demifling. No kissing, except for the occasional peck, almost always on the cheek, and almost always in public. Contact outside the sheltering walls of Valley Medical Center? Verboten. If a hand slipped beneath an untucked shirt, it never stayed there for more than an instant.

But Johnnie's restraint fell flat the moment she met Mr. Badenhaus. The first hint of disaster came just two weeks into our nonaffair, when a dapper man in a three-piece suit smiled and waved at Johnnie as he trotted by the *C* ward counter with a package under his arm.

"Who's that?" I asked. He seemed ordinary—short, stocky, his face round and plain as a dinner plate—but he wore the first three-piece suit I had seen on our charity ward.

"Oh," Johnnie said, "that's Jim." She caught herself and gave me a guilty glance. We weren't meant to refer to our patients or their family members by first names. "Jim Badenhaus," she said. "Big Momma's husband."

She blushed and said nothing more. That afternoon I caught Johnnie and Mr. Badenhaus together in the stairwell at the end of *C* ward. She stood leaning against a handrail, dragging on a cigarette, while he sat on a step with his hands in his lap. Did their startled glances hint at conspiracy? No one spoke. I trotted up the stairs, my pulse quickened by a jealous surge of adrenalin.

Then Ike got into the act. George Eikenboom, the senior resident on the blue team, whose narrow shoulders bore the burden of Big Momma's festering ulcer. The man was thin and jumpy, a chronic nervous wreck. He pitched a blazing row with Mr. Badenhaus when an orderly found a heart-shaped box on Big Momma's bedside table—a pound of See's chocolates, caramel cream stuffed with almonds and pecans, already half empty. Turns out the husband was bringing her a fresh box every day. Ike pounced on him.

"Jesus Christ, man," he said. "Four hundred pounds of infected fat—who the hell's side are you on?"

Johnnie laughed as she told this story, but her eyelashes glittered with tears. She blew her nose. I put my arm around her shoulders.

"Oh, fooey, I'm OK," she said, slamming an elbow into my ribs. She trotted away and locked herself in the drug room. The next day, a chrome-plated urinal filled with roses sat on the ward counter.

"My goodness, Johnnie," I said, "who's your lover?"

"Lover, hell." She gave me a sullen half-smile. "It was Mr. Badenhaus. After that row with Ike, he starts bringing roses instead of candy. Heads right into her room the second visiting hours begin, then runs out and gives me the old flowers wrapped in newspaper. Clicks his heels and bows like a prince. Makes me so mad I could spit."

"You're mad because some guy gives you used flowers? They don't look bad."

"Gamel," she whispered, her tone low, conspiratorial. I leaned across the counter. "He's a perfectly decent man."

"What?"

"The man's wonderful. A fine haircut. That suit—with a vest—hasn't got a spot on it. His nails are clean. You should smell his cologne. He's a true gentleman."

Johnnie thought she knew a lot about men. She had met her last husband on the ENT ward, nursed him through throat cancer, got him off booze, but he kept right on smoking three packs a day. One night while she was on duty, his bed caught fire and almost burned up their apartment. Now she lived alone.

* * *

After my surgery rotation, I began a month on pediatrics. A shock to the system: one day I was caring for swollen alcoholics and wheezing, blue-faced smokers, the next day innocent children. Things got off to a bad start. A young Hispanic couple became alarmed when their month-old son no longer took the breast with his usual vigor. To my unlearned eye, the kid looked healthy, an olive-skinned cherub with a button nose and a shock of black hair, perhaps sleepier than most. Yes, he seemed lethargic, and a trace of jaundice showed around his brown irises. When I laid my stethoscope on his chest and pressed my fingers on his soft belly, I found nothing out of the ordinary, but his blood tests showed multiorgan failure: liver, kidneys, pancreas—all dangerously inflamed.

This infant added a dimension to my universe. Looking into the dark, tragic eyes of the parents, I saw what love in its deepest measure is all about. Almost children themselves, they wanted nothing in the world but that their son should live. The night of his admission, I threaded a needle into a vein on the top of the infant's tiny foot, drew blood, then ran the latest test results up to my resident. He sat in the hospital library poring over journals, searching for a diagnosis and, with any luck, a treatment. At midnight he called the chief of pediatrics to report the child's amylase was dangerously high, his urine output falling every hour.

Mine were routine tasks, demanding little skill and no intellect, but during the hours I labored at their son's bedside, the parents came to see me as their saviour. The wild, staring terror drained from their faces, the eyes that followed my every move glowed with a calm and trusting spirit. I consumed their faith like a draft, but in the end it cost me a broken heart.

Ten p.m. Forty hours without sleep. I briefed the intern on duty that night, introduced him to the parents, then told them the simple truth—I must go home. Their faces showed the price I had to pay: moment by moment, as the meaning of my words took hold, the fear returned. Their faces fell. The mother slumped against the father's shoulder and wept. A few minutes later, while I sat at the ward counter writing my final notes of the evening, the father touched my shoulder. His hand was small and delicate, like the hand of a child. I looked up at the boyish face, the olive skin, the dark, pleading eyes.

"I must speak with you," he said. I winced from the pain of his tearful smile. "My wife…she prays…you must not go."

I did go home but slept badly. By morning the child was dead. The autopsy confirmed peritonitis with massive organ failure, but the cultures and histology slides came back negative. Two weeks later, a pathologist at Stanford finally looked at the electron micrographs, and there lay the answer, hidden among the ominous black dots and lines that spelled the end of a human life: toxoplasmosis. The cysts were scattered everywhere, melting the liver and kidneys into useless pulp. My resident called the family, and yes, the grandmother had a cat. The cat had kittens. A litter box alive with spores had killed their firstborn son. I had failed to ask the right question, missed the telltale clues, but antibiotics had only a limited effect on toxoplasmosis, and during that era no quick method could secure a diagnosis. The child was doomed the instant I saw him. That's the story I tell myself, even to this day.

And that's the story I told my wife the night after the infant died. I needed…well, something. She said nothing. She marked her place, laid her book on the table, sat beside me on the sofa, and took my hand. We sat for a long time. I needed to sob. I needed her arms around me, my head cradled between her breasts, but that, I knew, would never happen.

* * *

All this while, Big Momma's wound continued to fester. Ike finally bundled together her lab results and Kodachromes of the ulcer and presented them at

Stanford's surgical grand rounds. The case caused a riot. The Stanford faculty chewed out Ike for waiting so long, then voted for a panniculectomy—amputating the infected apron of fat that hung down to Big Momma's knees.

The operation turned into a saga fit for *The Annals of Surgery*. An engineer from the biomedical department bolted two operating tables together. Since fat soaks up anesthetic agents as readily as the brain, it took a massive dose of halothane to put Mrs. Badenhaus under. A resident and an intern scrubbed Big Momma's belly with Phisohex and Betadine for an hour, hoping to keep the soupy ulcer from contaminating the wound left after the amputation. Finally, in desperation, they used bone wire and huge autopsy needles to hoist her panniculus out of the way by tying it to an overhead light fixture and then sliced it off at the base with a sterilized autopsy knife. A pathology resident I met in the cafeteria said the specimen was shipped down from the OR in a trash can. He claimed it weighed almost forty pounds.

Big Momma's fat cells retained so much halothane it took her two days to wake up. The recovery-room supervisor swore that all that time, Mr. Badenhaus sat beside his wife's bed, pressing her limp hand against his cheek.

* * *

After my pediatric rotation, I looked forward to a happy reunion with Johnnie, but when I found her walking alone down a dark hallway, she resisted my hug—stiffened in my arms and backed away. I thought her interest in Big Momma's husband had run its course, but I was wrong.

Later that night, over cups of scorched coffee in the deserted cafeteria, Johnnie told her awful story. Soon after I left for my pediatric rotation, she and Mr. Badenhaus began meeting for breakfast at a nearby Waffle House. One morning, over plates of sausage and pancakes, she declared her undying love for him, and he responded—or so she swore—with equal passion. It was just a matter of time, perhaps a week or two after his wife's discharge, until all would be settled.

"But Johnnie," I said, "that's terrible. Ridiculous. You're a nurse, for God's sake. If the California medical board finds out, they'll pull your license."

"Don't be so narrow-minded," she said, scowling and leaning across the table to stare me in the eye. A cigarette smoldered between her fingers. Her fake lashes were absurdly long. The bluish fluorescent light showed the crow's feet at the corners of her eyes. She took a slow, meditative drag, then turned her head to exhale. "Jim's a wonderful man. And you know damn well he deserves better than that creature…that…that beached whale. We've been careful, very discreet."

"Let me wish the lucky couple all the happiness in the world," I said, struggling to control the quaver in my voice. Her rejection, her stiffening against my embrace, had infuriated me. "Have you two love birds done the deed?"

"What deed?"

"Oh, you know," I said, pinching my left thumb and forefinger into a circle, then poking my right forefinger rhythmically in and out of the hole.

She—"Ouch!"—kicked me under the table.

"Of course not. He's not that kind of man."

But I soon discovered Johnnie had only seduced herself. The two of them had never laid a hand on each other. When Johnnie blurted "I love you," Badenhaus, driven by politeness or confusion, let slip the fatal words, "I love you, too." Now the woods were on fire.

It ended badly. The man adored his enormous wife, had always adored her, cherished her every crease and every pendulous fold. Those deep-set eyes were heaven to him. Betrayal was the last thing on his mind, even though his beloved lay stuporous from morphine, her body fouled by a ragged, gaping wound. If he loved Johnnie, it was only because she took care of his wife and kept him company during the lonely morning hours. But Johnnie was a fool when it came to matters of the heart. Having suffered a string of faithless lovers, she treasured loyalty like a jewel, and never had she seen such marital devotion as that shown by the man she hoped to lure astray.

I don't know what Mr. Badenhaus finally said to straighten her out, but one night I found Johnnie fuming behind the *C* ward counter. My "What's up?" brought an explosion.

"That creep Badenhaus," she growled, her face dark with rage. "He thinks he's king of the world, wants to sit there holding that beached whale's hand all night long. 'No way,' I told him. 'Visiting hours here are eight a.m. to eight p.m.'"

"But Johnnie," I said, "how could you—after all those flowers?"

She snarled and shook her fist at me.

"He can take those and stick 'em you know where. I'm boss around here, and I don't put up with that kind of crap on my shift. If I let that son of a bitch get away with it, then every sleazebag on the ward is gonna want her sweetheart to sit there rubbing her feet or maybe her pussy 'til the sun comes up."

* * *

Big Momma's love triangle had collapsed, probably without her knowing anything about it, but her recovery was far from over. Five days after surgery, the stitches fell out. The wound festered and gaped like a cave. Ike switched her IV antibiotics from gentamycin to ampicillin and repacked the cavity twice a day with four pounds of gauze. Week after week, her 1500-calorie diet melted away the fat. Two months later, when the last inch of her wound finally healed, she weighed just under 300 pounds.

Her discharge from the hospital turned into a celebration. At the end of the dayshift, the *C* ward staff crowded into a conference room on the rehab wing. There were balloons, flowers, and a muscular gentleman in a tuxedo who stripped down to a g-string while gyrating and lip-synching a hip-hop version of "You Ain't Nothin' but a Hound Dog" that blared from a portable tape player. Ike let Mrs. Badenhaus eat a piece of the chocolate cake her husband had made. Fifteen candles burned in a circle, one for every ten pounds she had lost during her stay.

But this was not the end of Big Momma's story. Later her husband admitted that on their way home from the hospital, they had stopped to buy a case of Coors and a KFC family bucket. It took her only three months to gain back a hundred pounds. The panniculus bulged out tense as a pregnant belly. The scar broke down and ulcerated. The day my internship ended, Mrs. Badenhaus lay in her old double bed, an IV drip in her arm, staring up at the ceiling with morphine-glazed eyes.

By that time, Johnnie had transferred to the orthopedics ward at Stanford. During the three years of my residency, I saw her several times in the hospital cafeteria, but she met my gaze with cold, unfriendly eyes. We never spoke again.

* * *

Romance is a strange business, especially when it lasts. I've always been drawn by the icon of physical beauty. My wife was thin, cool, astringent, and to me—perhaps only to me—the loveliest of women. I emphasize "was." After a decade of marriage, she gagged every time I touched her. I haven't seen her in thirty years. One day while Big Momma's husband and I chatted outside her room, he mentioned that on his wedding night, he had massaged his wife's feet. She was heavy even then, and all that weight tears hell out of the arches. This nightly ritual had endured for twenty years. I remembered my Russian émigré and his puffy-faced wife: drinking like fish, shouting and fighting and ugly as sin, they had stuck it out to the end. Night after night, all over the world, ugly people lie down together in the same bed, sharing their lives until one of them dies.

CHAPTER NINE

The Sleepers

Of all the patients I cared for during my internship, one group holds a special place in my memory. I call them the sleepers—patients who lay motionless for days or weeks at a time, their eyes closed and their arms resting peacefully at their sides. These were my greatest burdens, yet caring for them gave me a transcendent sense of power. Day after day, I attended to their every need, with no clue from the souls who dwelled inside those still and silent bodies.

Maria Gonzales, the most beautiful of my sleepers, was six years old when I admitted her to the neurosurgery service. She had dark eyes and magnificent dark hair, but fate is seldom swayed by beauty. Vomiting and terrible headaches had brought her to the hospital. My examination revealed choked discs, swelling of the optic nerves caused by high intracranial pressure. Adrianna, the unmarried aunt who brought Maria to the hospital, sat alone at the bedside for hours every day, her face radiant with tenderness as she stroked the girl's hair, fluffed her pillow, held a cup of water to her lips. I learned from a social worker that Maria's parents had deserted her soon after her birth.

The neurosurgery team had only an intern, a resident named Ron Goldstein, and a tall, gaunt attending who had retired from the navy some years before. Ron and I called him the Admiral. He carried a meerschaum pipe and often chewed on the stem, though the pipe was seldom lit. When Maria's cerebral angiogram was done, Ron laid out her films on a view box. After a long, morbid silence, the Admiral spoke.

"Christ—look at that tumor blush in the left parietal lobe. It has to be glioblastoma."

"Yup," Ron said. "Glioblastoma. No doubt about it."

"We'd better start the Solu-Medrol," the Admiral said. "How much?"

"Let's try a hundred milligrams a day."

We had nothing to say. The child was doomed. Solu-Medrol, a powerful synthetic cortisone infused through a vein, would lower her intracranial pressure and relieve her headaches for a while, but no treatment known to medicine could stop the tumor. It would soon devour the poor girl's brain.

Maria's headaches vanished. For two weeks, she ran up and down the pediatric ward and spent hours watching TV and trading soft toys with the other kids in the playroom. Every evening, Adrianna set the child on her lap to read a bedtime story. When the headaches returned, Ron and I worked out the dosage of IV morphine needed to control her pain, but this made her drowsy, and soon she took to her bed. Adrianna now kept a round-the-clock vigil.

The nightmare seemed to go on and on. One morning while examining Maria, I discovered lumps in her neck. The Admiral gently felt the lumps and shook his head in amazement.

"I've never seen this before—the tumor has metastasized outside her skull."

Two days later, Adrianna gave us more devastating news.

"Maria doesn't wake up very often, but when she does, she says the headache is terrible, and she claims she can't see anything."

The Admiral, his face grim as death, opened Maria's lids with his fingers and shined a flashlight into each eye. The light did not arouse the girl. Her enormous pupils remained fixed and dilated.

"Yes," he said, "I'm afraid the child is blind."

Adrianna stood motionless, staring ahead as though blind herself. Silent tears flowed down her cheeks. The Admiral gave her a hug. He seemed ready to speak again, then removed his arm from her shoulder. Ron and I followed him down the hall to a conference room. He waited for us to enter, then closed the door.

"Well," the Admiral said, settling into a chair, "the Solu-Medrol doesn't seem to be working. We might as well stop it."

"Yup," Ron said. "That sounds like a good plan. I'll write the order."

Something about the idea bothered me. I probed my memory, seeking a fragment retained from a textbook or a lecture.

"Ah, but wait," I said. "Surely you don't mean we should stop it all at once. That whopping dose of Solu-Medrol has shut down her adrenals. If we just cut it off cold, her blood pressure will drop like a rock. Shouldn't we taper off the dosage to let her adrenals recover?"

It was a proud moment. I had dredged up a gem, an erudite fact to save my mentors from a dangerous lapse in their reasoning, but Ron and the Admiral didn't thank me. They gazed at me in silence. Perhaps they were embarrassed by their lapse or impressed by my precocious knowledge. The Admiral lit his pipe, took a few puffs, grunted to himself, and shook his head. Ron turned red in the face.

"Jesus Christ, Gamel," he said. "How dumb can a man get? Did your mother have any children that lived?"

The Admiral's plan worked. Ron discontinued the Solu-Medrol, and over the next thirty-six hours, Maria's blood pressure fell lower and lower. She died without regaining consciousness.

* * *

Granny Simpson, a seventy-year-old widow, distinguished herself as my most bizarre sleeper. During the course of a week, she worked her way through a cascade of life-threatening disasters, all the while urging us to stop the treatments and let her die. Even her family opted for death, arguing that Granny had suffered enough.

It started one night when ambulance attendants pulled Granny from her wrecked Cadillac and brought her to our ER. She had ruptured her spleen on the steering wheel. Lancy Allen, my senior resident, scheduled her for emergency surgery, then typed and cross-matched six units of blood, but getting Granny to the OR proved an uphill battle. She refused to sign the consent form, insisting that she was a worn-out old woman with nothing left to live for. Soon her two grown children showed up and gave Lancy the same story: Granny had been depressed for years, insisting time and again she would be better off dead. Why not let nature take its course?

Lancy was at his wits' end. Since Granny smelled of liquor and had suffered a major trauma, she couldn't make a rational decision. The family kept telling us the old lady was worn out and ready to die, yet before the wreck, she had been in perfect health except for her depression. When Lancy called the hospital's lawyer, he said we should go ahead with surgery. To do otherwise, he insisted, would be nothing less than mercy killing.

So we hauled Granny off to the OR kicking and screaming. Her surgery proved a close shave. The ruptured spleen had dumped pints of blood into her abdomen, dropping her blood pressure to a critical level, where it stayed until the anesthesiologist gave her several transfusions. The attending surgeon thought her liver was enlarged, suggesting alcohol abuse. Lancy wouldn't buy it. True, she had liquor on her breath, but she was well-dressed when brought into the ER, and her children seemed solid members of the upper class.

Indeed, Granny didn't look like a typical alcoholic, but on her third post-op day, she went into florid delirium tremens. By the time a generous dose of IV Valium brought her hallucinations under control, she turned blue and began gasping for breath. A stat pulmonary consult diagnosed shock lung caused by the prolonged drop in her blood pressure.

For any hope of survival, I had to put her on a respirator, but she would have nothing of it. After she pulled out her endotracheal tube three times, an anesthesia resident helped me set up a curare drip to keep her paralyzed twenty-four hours a day. This turned Granny into a special type of sleeper. She was awake yet couldn't move a muscle, couldn't even open her eyes, lying still as a corpse except for the rise and fall of her chest in rhythm with the *hiss...clunk...hiss...clunk* of the respirator. Her children visited the ICU every day. Now their protests reached a fever pitch.

"Poor Granny, why do you keep tormenting her like this? Why don't you let the old lady have her way? She's miserable and wants to die."

Every other day, Lancy was on the phone to the hospital's lawyer, who still insisted that so long as there was any chance for a full recovery, we should do all we could to save her. It mattered not that she and her family fought our every move.

A week after these disasters began, Granny's lungs cleared up. Rather than the corpse she had hoped for, she was a healthy woman, sober and clear-eyed, with no tremors and a recovering liver. Best of all, we could stop the curare drip. The moment we took her off the respirator, allowing her to speak, Lancy and I were astonished to find ourselves heroes. She grabbed my arm every time I came near her bed.

"Oh, Doctor," Granny said, "thank you so much. I just can't tell you how grateful I am. You saved me, and it's wonderful to be alive. I've never felt better in my life."

Her family proved even more effusive. They brought a huge basket of fruit for the ICU staff and sent a card to Lancy and me, a flowery message thanking us for saving their beloved mother. Most memorable of all was the gratitude shown by one granddaughter, a young woman with long blonde hair who visited the ICU wearing a halter top and skin-tight denim shorts. One night she grabbed me in the hall outside the ICU, stunned me with a hug that cracked my ribs, and then rose on tiptoes to whisper in my ear. Our cheeks touched. She would do anything, anything in the world, to show her gratitude.

I've forgotten my mumbled reply, but I remember Lancy's outrage when he heard of the encounter from an ICU nurse.

"You selfish jerk," he said. "I'm the surgeon, the one who saved the old girl's life. If you had a decent bone in your body, you'd tell that babe she ought to be hugging up on me. Besides, I'm single, and you're married."

In the end, the story fell short of a fairy tale. I kept in touch with Granny's daughter, the mother of the affectionate granddaughter, and she told me that for two months after Granny's discharge, she seemed to have a new lease on life. The old lady took up golf, joined AA, and began keeping company with a widower who lived next door in an upscale apartment near San Mateo. Then she fell off the wagon. A few weeks later, the manager evicted her for drunk and disorderly conduct. The last I heard, she was the oldest resident in a rehab center run by the Salvation Army.

* * *

Greg Caraway was a forty-five-year-old pilot who lived in Cupertino, a few miles from the San Jose Airport. When he developed progressive nausea, fatigue, and depression, his private doctor admitted him to a private hospital. According to the records, the doctor found no abnormalities on physical exam, but he described the patient as "lethargic and confused." He ordered a battery of tests, then went home for a good night's sleep. The next morning, all the lab tests were normal, but he was disturbed to find his patient obtunded, almost comatose. The doctor considered all the relevant information, including the fact that the Memorial Day weekend was coming soon, and dispatched Greg to Santa Clara Valley Medical Center, where I admitted him to the medical ICU.

The first time I saw Greg, he inspired a strange thought: *How could anyone give up such a beautiful patient?* Not that he was terribly handsome, but lying in coma, his arms resting at his sides, he seemed beatific, his face an embodiment of peace and repose. The ICU nurses often stood by his bed, gazing in wonder at his seraphic features. I examined Greg from head to toe and found no abnormality except for his coma. Walter O'Conner, my resident on the medicine service, had no better luck. Together we looked through the records sent over from the private hospital.

"Damn," Walter said, "here's an EKG, but there's no report."

"Ah, too bad," I said, but my own heart throbbed with excitement. During a cardiology elective, I had learned to read EKGs, and the tracing showed marked shortening of the QT interval and a prolongation of the T wave. These were obvious signs of hypercalcemia, an elevated serum calcium, which can lead to depression and coma. What a treat—Walter had missed the clue!

Rather than tell him of my suspicion, I waited for a lab test of Greg's serum calcium. This was not included in routine lab tests during that era, but I convinced the pathologist to run a stat assay, and two hours later, report in hand, I thrust my finding under Walter's nose.

"Hey, look at this," I said. "Caraway's calcium is off the scale. That's what put him in a coma."

Walter glanced at the slip, then glowered at me. I was delighted to see that my brilliant coup and obnoxious grin had pissed him off.

"Well, smartass," he said, "you got any idea what's causing this?"

"Uh...no, I don't."

"And treatment—any thoughts on that?"

"Uh...no."

"Then you'd better get busy."

Walter and I were pleased by what we found in *The Merck Manual of Diagnosis and Therapy*, which showed a long list of possible causes for hypercalcemia. Most were benign or amenable to treatment. Perhaps Greg had overactive parathyroid glands. Perhaps he suffered from an inherited disease or had taken too much vitamin D or too many antacid tablets. The list also included disseminated cancer, which could dissolve the calcium in a patient's bones, but the tests done so far had revealed no hint of malignancy. A few hours later, our optimism collapsed when a radiologist paged Walter with devastating news. Greg's X-rays showed hundreds of dark spots scattered through his skull, ribs, and spine. The poor man was doomed.

This left us with only one question: where had these tumors come from? We requested consults from oncology, gastroenterology, and urology. In the end, the urology resident found the answer. After his first exam, he pronounced Greg's prostate unremarkable, but the next morning I found him back at Greg's bedside.

"I lay awake half the night thinking about this guy," he said. "Since the textbooks say those mets most likely came from his prostate, I decided to take another look, and this time I convinced myself things don't feel quite right. There's no obvious lump, but I don't like the texture of the left lobe. I'll be back this afternoon for a needle biopsy."

Bingo. The next day, I was charting at the ICU desk when a clerk delivered the report from the biopsy. Greg had cancer of the prostate. It proved a terrible moment. Twenty feet away, his wife and two teenagers stood beside his gurney, gazing down at his peaceful face. The wife was a frail, anxious woman with dark circles under her eyes. I dreaded the speech I had to give: *Ma'am, I'm afraid we've got some news, and it's not good....* No, I had a better idea. I paged Walter and told him about the biopsy.

"Look," I said, "I had to tell Greg's wife about the mets in his bones. Now it's your turn." A few minutes later, he arrived in the ICU, gave me a look that said I was a rotten coward and would owe him big time, then led Greg's wife down the hall to the hospital chapel.

Would that this had been the end of Greg's story. What we needed to do was obvious—let the poor man die in peace—but an enemy leapt upon us.

* * *

During my years at Stanford, the oncology department proved both famous and notorious, a collection of brilliant lunatics. They won millions of dollars in research grants and published dozens of papers in prestigious journals. But at their worst, they tormented cancer patients with a consuming and irrational passion, a passion that often served only to prolong hopeless misery. Dr. X, the department's chairman, was so aggressive in his treatments, a dark jest haunted him throughout his tenure: Dr. X rushes to a graveside just as the pallbearers lower the coffin. "Wait! Wait!" he shouts. "There's still time for one more dose of 5-FU." Five-fluorouracyl is a toxic drug used to treat advanced malignancies.

When we first discovered the cancer in Greg's bones, an oncology fellow from Stanford had answered our request for a consult. Trained by Dr. X and his minions, he did a thorough job, listing all the sites from which the tumor might have spread and all the tests we needed to order. He also gave us a protocol for bringing George out of his coma by lowering the serum calcium, but with no hope for a cure, we decided to let nature take its course. A few days later, when Walter paged me to the ICU, I found him fuming.

"What happened?" I asked.

"It's that asshole from Stanford—the oncology fellow. He came back for a follow-up exam and chewed me out. Called me a terrible doctor, threatened to sue me for malpractice."

"My God!" I said. "What the hell is he talking about?"

"He insists we have to treat Greg's hypercalcemia, pull out all the stops so we can wake him up."

"Wow!" I said, buoyed by a surge of optimism. "You mean they've found something new, a drug that might wipe out all of Greg's mets?"

"Hell no. That moron made it clear—there's nothing new for prostate cancer, nothing at all. They're still stuck with 5-FU, but this guy wants us to start pouring it in right now. Maybe it'll shrink the tumors by 50 percent, but only if we give whopping doses. The best we can hope for is a few weeks, a month or two at best."

I stared at Walter. My brain struggled to take in this lunacy.

"Wait a minute," I said. "They want us to wake the man up so we can tell him he's a goner, tell him he'll spend his last few days of life writhing in pain from his tumors and puking up his guts from the 5-FU?"

"Yeah, that's what he told me to do."

Despite the oncologist's rant, all went well in the end. Walter sat down with the ICU director and worked out a protocol. We gave Greg intravenous diuretics and calcitonin, the standard treatment for hypercalcemia, plus a few milligrams of 5-FU, but the doses weren't enough to do the job. I wrote a standby order for IV morphine in case he woke up screaming with pain, but it was never needed. Greg remained in a coma for five days, his face calm and peaceful as a sleeping baby's. He died without stirring a limb.

* * *

My most prestigious sleeper was Michael B., a ten-year-old whose father had been the mayor of San Jose and the head of the county school board. The trouble began when a pediatrician treated Michael with aspirin for what seemed a typical case of influenza. He complained of a headache, developed severe nausea and vomiting, then was admitted to a private hospital for intravenous rehydration. At midnight, a nurse called the pediatrician to report that Michael's urine output had dropped to almost nothing. He had also become confused and disoriented. These symptoms gave the final clue: Michael had Reye's syndrome, a mysterious affliction that devastates the brain and other vital organs. There was no proven treatment. The pediatrician, reluctant to spend fruitless hours at the bedside of a doomed child, shipped Michael to Valley Medical Center.

At three a.m., as attendants transferred him to a bed in the ICU, I introduced myself to the parents. All three of us had been up for thirty or forty hours. We sagged from exhaustion, but they had managed to dress for the occasion in a suit and a stylish dress, as though on their way to church, while I wore rumpled OR scrubs. Michael lay a few feet away, a beloved golden-haired child, but he already had the jaundiced skin and urinelike stench brought on by liver failure. The father was so distracted, I had to repeat my questions two or three times before he could muster an answer. The mother remained silent. Again and again, they turned to watch the ICU nurses as they tucked the boy into bed and attended to his IV. He was delirious, screaming at the nurses, flailing his arms and legs in a wild struggle. I had attended a lecture on Reye's syndrome during medical school and knew the dreadful truth: soon, the boy would be in a deep coma.

In 1962, Doctor Douglas Reye, an attending at the Royal Alexandra Hospital for Children in New South Wales, Australia, described twenty-one cases of a mysterious disease. All had occurred in children who suffered from what initially seemed a routine viral illness, such as influenza or chicken pox. Over the course of hours or days, they became delirious, fell into a stupor, then developed liver failure and renal shutdown. Seventeen of the victims died. Of those who survived, most had permanent afflictions, including cirrhosis, brain damage, and chronic renal failure. Doctor Reye, noting that all the autopsies showed profound swelling of the brain, liver, and kidneys, called the disease fatty degeneration of the viscera.

This paper was published ten years before Michael's illness, and in the interim no cure had been found. Thus, when the boy entered our ICU, all we knew was that he would soon suffer total organ shutdown, and his odds of survival remained slim. The best we could offer were educated guesses.

An hour after Michael's admission, I saw a grey-haired man approach his bed. The stranger was dressed in street clothes, but when he pulled a stethoscope from his pocket, I realized he must be a doctor. This was Joseph Garvey, a senior attending on the pediatric service. A few minutes later, in an office across the hall from the ICU, he explained to my resident and me what we should do for Michael. To keep his kidneys working, he needed diuretics. To maintain hydration, he needed intravenous fluids. Most important of all, we should give intravenous cortisone to reduce the swelling in his brain.

From their dour expressions and subdued voices, I knew that neither Garvey nor my resident expected the boy to survive. Reye's syndrome was a cruel, inscrutable beast that devoured organs one by one, transforming a healthy child into a bloated corpse in a matter of days. Depressed and exhausted, I wrote out the orders, then, while the nurses infused the appropriate fluids and medicines into Michael's veins, I explained our plans to the parents. Garvey had warned me not to give them false hope, but there was no danger of that. Their crestfallen faces made it clear they expected their son to die.

Perhaps fate was in a good mood that day. Perhaps Michael, unaware of the odds against him, decided not to die. Twelve hours after we began our treatment, he woke from his coma. His jaundice cleared. His kidneys poured pints of urine into the bag hanging at the foot of his bed. A few days later, his mind was intact, his blue eyes bright and clear.

The morning of Michael's discharge, his parents ambushed me. They bought a box of candy at the gift shop and had the page operator summon me to the discharge desk. Weary from a night on call, I stumbled downstairs to answer the call. The mother offered me the box, but the moment I took it, she threw her arms around me. I struggled against her embrace, trying to explain it was all a mistake—I was just the gofer, a glorified errand boy—but she would have none of it. Doctor Garvey had been the brains behind it all, yet I was the one who had labored night after night at their son's bedside. Before I could break from the mother's grip, the father embraced both of us, pressing his cheek against mine. Tears flowed from their eyes, so many tears I wept myself. Michael sat nearby in a wheelchair. His face blushed, but he kept quiet until the blubbering died down. When everyone had blown their noses and dried their eyes, he stood up from the chair and grasped my hand.

"Thanks, Doctor Gamel," he said. "I was always glad to see you, especially at night. Don't you guys ever get to sleep?"

* * *

Of all the advice I've given and received during my medical career, this dictum remains my favorite: if your fairy godmother wakes you in the night to offer a choice between great skill and great luck, take the luck. In defense of this philosophy, I present the case of Michael B. The history of Reye's syndrome shows the vital role simple-minded pragmatism can play in the practice of medicine. Over the decades after Doctor Reye published his famous paper, studies showed that almost all the victims had been given aspirin early in the course of a viral illness. Though theories abound, to this day no one has discovered the mechanism by which aspirin interacts with a viral infection to destroy every vital organ in the body. Yet despite our ignorance, an international campaign to avoid the use of aspirin for treating febrile illnesses in children has all but eliminated Reye's syndrome.

As for treatment, pragmatism again saved the day. There is still no specific cure, but now doctors know what to do—use common sense. The victims all suffer from dehydration and renal failure and swelling of the brain, thus we should give them IV fluids and diuretics and cortisone. Studies conducted since Michael's illness show that these simple measures, if performed early in the course of the disease, dramatically improve the odds of recovery.

Since that desperate night when Doctor Garvey devised Michael's treatment, guided by principles known even then to a third-year medical student, his plan remains the gold standard forty years later. Experience has shown that if we can sustain the victim's vital functions, the mysterious disease will run its course without destroying the delicate intracellular structures that sustain life. Thus a few simple measures have spared thousands of children from the ravages of Reye's syndrome. As with many maladies over the course of human history, when science failed, luck and common sense saved the day. We also owe this triumph to prior defeats: the tragic losses of the parents who allowed Doctor Reye to study the bodies of their dead children.

CHAPTER TEN

Larry Beaten

The closest I have ever come to surrendering my skepticism—the one time I was most tempted to look heavenward and say, "OK, God, you sardonic old wag, you win"—must be credited to a patient who arrived one rainy Saturday night at the Valley Medical Center. Since the circumstances of this case now shield me from the laws governing libel and confidentiality, I can reveal his real name: Larry Beaten. He'd been beaten half to death. In the end, his story would prove as tragic and bizarre as his name.

I was the intern on call for neurosurgery when an ambulance delivered Larry's motionless body to the ER. His clothes smelled of vomit and his curly brown hair was matted with blood, but he had a good pulse, fair color, and moaned when I twisted the flat handle of a reflex hammer between two tightly squeezed toes. If I twisted until the toes cracked, he opened his eyes and weakly flailed both arms and legs, but then, the instant the pain ceased, he lapsed back into a stupor. I rated him eight out of fifteen on the Glasgow Coma Scale— halfway between normal and dead.

Larry's history trickled in bit by bit. His California driver's license declared him a twenty-nine-year-old Caucasian male. When the ambulance driver told an ER clerk that Larry had been picked up off the floor at Melanie's Grill, a San Jose nightspot famous for its drunken brawls, the clerk called Melanie's and handed me the phone. For several minutes I listened to a running debate on the other end of the line between a bartender and a drunken patron: Larry's assailants—there were two; no, three, maybe four—had come after him with their fists. And there was a chair, plus a bottle or two, slammed upside his head. The fight had begun when Larry spat in someone's beer.

The physical evidence confirmed this story. The ER intern who sewed up Larry's scalp lacerations found bits of broken glass embedded in the wounds, while tense black bruises on the occiput and left cheek suggested blunt trauma. The skull X-ray showed no acute fracture, though hypertrophic lines suggested one or two healed fractures. In any case, Larry's contused brain was taking a rest. Judging by the old fractures—plus seven scars on his scalp and face, one of which ran from the corner of his right eye to the angle of his jaw—I suspected his brain had taken several such rests in the past.

* * *

Ron Goldstein, the resident who dispatched me to look after Larry, was an arrogant, difficult man. Years later, when he became the chairman of neurosurgery at a preeminent medical school, his tenure was marred by an infamous locking of horns with America's most celebrated female neurosurgeon. During an interview publicized by the media, she declared Ron the quintessential male chauvinist pig. In fact, Ron gave everyone a hard time—men and women, young and old, doctors and nurses, even the occasional patient—but I loved him. Yes, he could be a jerk. His sense of humor was caustic, merciless, riotously brilliant. He was a brilliant man altogether, almost as skilled a surgeon and diagnostician as he claimed to be.

When the Stanford ophthalmology department accepted me as a resident, Ron clapped me on the shoulder. "Congratulations, Gamel," he said in a loud voice. "If you can't be a real doctor, you might as well fit eyeglasses for the rest of your life." He often spoke in a loud voice. When a medical student announced that he wanted to become an internist, Ron harangued him: "You lazy bastard, that'll break your mother's heart. A good Jewish boy like you should get off his ass and become a surgeon." In the cafeteria one day, apropos of nothing in particular, Ron all but shouted, "Pediatricians are the biggest wimps on earth. Not a one of them has a peter any bigger than a cigarette." The pediatricians sitting at the next table fell silent and turned red in the face.

But Ron was a superb physician. If my brain harbored a meningioma, I would place myself in his hands without a moment's hesitation. Beneath the anger and raucous humor there dwelt an abiding integrity—an integrity at times conflicted, to be sure, yet fierce and unrelenting.

It was this integrity, not Ron's swollen ego, that cost two innocent victims their lives.

* * *

Where did Ron's anger and smoldering hostility come from? His grey eyes were piercing, defiant, as though daring anyone to look askance at his limping stride. That he was handsome, with broad shoulders and a strong, classic jaw, only added to the response his frown and peculiar gait aroused in strangers. Stares followed him whenever we walked the corridors of Valley Medical Center. Ron seemed to sense these stares, scowling while his deformed legs struggled to leave them behind as quickly as possible. His limp, I soon discovered, had much to do with his hatred of drunks.

Yes, Ron hated drunks. This never affected the quality of his care—he gave excellent care to all his patients, poring over their charts and X-rays into the early morning hours—but at the bedside of a lush, he uttered not one word more than was needed. These were dark little sessions, with a stuporous, slack-jawed patient struggling to tell his story while Ron glowered at him and clenched his teeth. In the ER, amid the reek of vomit and infected wounds, or in the ICU, sonorous with the *hiss...clunk... hiss...clunk* of half a dozen respirators, I often thought, *If the world agreed to look the other way for ten seconds, Ron would kill that man with his bare hands*. But Ron restrained himself.

"Sit up, dammit—I'm talking to you!"

Those were the harshest words I ever heard him speak to the drunkards that filled so many of the beds in our hospital. At rounds one evening, when Ron interrupted a gentle old alcoholic in the midst of a rambling confabulation by scowling at the poor man and telling him to shut up, I asked Ron where this anger came from. He led me to an empty room and sat down on a chair.

"Look," he said, snatching up the legs of his blue scrub trousers. "Lean down, get closer."

I leaned down. His shins were lumpy, covered with curly hair. Flecks of black pigment lay scattered beneath a lacework of scars.

"That asshole," Ron said. "A drunk Asian. He sold fortune cookies. It was Christmas, my first year of medical school. I was going to marry this beautiful girl. We were walking home from a movie, and the asshole ran over us. She was gone, killed on the spot, the murdering son of a bitch. He killed her and broke my legs. The black stuff is asphalt."

Since that day, every whiff of alcohol on a patient's breath inflamed the memory of his murdered bride-to-be, while every stride on those twisted legs was charged against the drunkards of the world. But Ron's integrity always held sway, even against a resentment that tainted every aspect of his life. If he denied alcoholics his respect or a cheerful smile, he never denied them the best care a doctor could give.

* * *

Pig Shit Collins had a well-earned nickname. At least once a month, our ER admitted a free spirit who had sailed through the windshield of his pickup truck, but Mr. Collins distinguished himself by landing in a pigsty.

He arrived combative and blind drunk, covered with a mixture of mud and pig feces. Two orderlies wheeled him to the cast room, stripped off his clothes, then hosed him down and left him strapped on a gurney so he could scream himself to sleep.

Collins probably would have died there if Ron G. hadn't stopped to chat with the patrolman who had worked the crash site. Ron got on well with cops, perhaps because they hated drunks as much as he did. He had seen Pig Shit cursing and swinging at the orderlies and gave no thought to a serious injury until the patrolman mentioned an alarming fact: the pigsty Mr. Collins had landed in was over a hundred feet from the wrecked pickup.

"Oh, Christ," Ron said. He rushed to the cast room with me on his heels. By that time, Collins had quieted down. He lay naked, shivering, whimpering under the wet sheet. "You OK?" Ron shouted in his ear.

"No," Collins moaned. His teeth chattered. He burst into choking sobs. "My neck hurts."

Ron's response amazed me. That pathetic moan— "My neck hurts"—transformed Ron's face, his posture, his tone of voice. One moment he seemed ready to squash Collins like a bug, the next he was tender and anxious as though caring for an injured child.

"Hurry up," Ron said to me as he kicked off the gurney's brakes and grabbed a side rail. "Let's get him to X-ray."

The PA and lateral films showed an undisplaced fracture of the odontoid process, the pivotal point of the upper cervical spine. Pig Shit Collins had broken his neck. If the fragment slipped, it would snap the spinal cord just below its exit from the skull. Collins, hovering a millimeter from instant death, had begun to sober up.

For the next hour, while Collins' gurney was trundled to radiology and then to the OR, Ron stayed by his side every instant. He kept a hand on the patient's brow to steady his head until the anesthetic took effect. When Collins awoke, his head was shaved smooth, and a plaster cast covered his upper torso. Four long vertical rods embedded in the cast joined a steel circle held in place by six pins driven into Collins' skull. This crown of thorns—seeming, to the unlearned eye, nothing more than a splendid instrument of torture—was designed to stabilize the spine while the fractured odontoid healed.

In the recovery room, Ron held Collins' hand as he regained consciousness.

"Yeah, I know it hurts," he said in a gentle voice, "but trust me, things will get better. You must not move. Just hang on; another shot of morphine will do the trick."

Our efforts on Collins' behalf were handsomely rewarded. The morning after surgery, bathed and shaved with special care—lest an untoward movement sever his spine—he showed himself a comely fellow. His naked scalp glowed like a porcelain doorknob. His pale blue eyes, framed by dark lashes, seemed innocent as a child's, painfully sweet and precious, while the crown of thorns gave him the heart-rending aura of a pieta.

No doubt such beauty had a moving effect on the two young women who rushed into his room the moment visiting hours began, each carrying a brown paper bag tucked under her arm. One was Collins' girlfriend, the other his wife. Within seconds, the bags were torn, their contents scattered across the floor: toothbrushes, flannel pajamas, a purple robe, and various foodstuffs broken into crumbs or mashed into greasy lumps.

Ron and I had just finished morning rounds at the other end of the hall when the two women tumbled out of Collins' room in a heap, both pounding away, shouting "Bitch! Bitch! Bitch!" at the top of their lungs. I had thought women only bit and scratched and pulled hair, but the thin, honey-gold blonde—I never found out whether she was the wife or the girlfriend—was admitted to ENT with a fractured mandible. Her opponent, a sturdy Hispanic woman, had scratches on her face and neck and a tooth-hole punched through her lower lip. After an ER intern stitched her lip, she sat by Collins' bed until visiting hours were over.

* * *

That evening, as Collins whimpered with pain from the six pins screwed into his skull, Larry Beaten took a turn for the worse. A nurse paged me after midnight to report that his coma had deepened. I checked him out. Bad news: a reflex hammer twisted between his toes until they cracked elicited only faint movements of his left arm and leg, while his right arm and leg lay motionless. He no longer moaned, and his eyes remained closed. These findings dropped his Glasgow Coma Scale to four out of fifteen points—near death. When I woke Ron, he ordered a stat skull film and a cerebral arteriogram, and by two a.m. the data were in: Larry had a subdural hematoma overlying his left frontal lobe. Ron sent me off to talk to the family while he prepared Larry for surgery.

"Be sure to hang some crepe," he said. "The poor schmuck might lose his frontal lobes, so you'd better give 'em that routine about a change in personality."

A lobotomy—caused by trauma, by an unintended operative complication, or by a deliberate surgical procedure—tends to soothe the savage beast. The procedure was developed in the 1930s to treat a variety of mental ailments, then reached its apogee a decade later when Doctor Walter Freeman pioneered his "ice-pick lobotomy." During this five-minute procedure, he hammered a slender rod into the brain through the bony wall of each eye socket and then waved the tip around to sever all neural connections with the frontal lobes. The patient remained wide awake. Eye drops served as the only anesthetic. For ten years, Doctor Freeman toured America in what he called his "lobotomobile," performing 3,439 operations, but this surgical travesty was abandoned during the 1970s because many of his victims—including Rose Marie Kennedy, John F. Kennedy's sister—became slovenly automatons. Ron feared that Larry's subdural hematoma, or the surgery to remove it, might lobotomize the patient. I had to prepare his family for this complication.

I looked forward to seeing Larry's family again. During my first meeting with them, on the night of his admission, I had developed a crush on his sister Virginia, a young woman with a narrow face and dark hair that shimmered under the fluorescent lights of the ICU. My heart carried a soft spot for thin, literate women, and the intellectual mien imparted by the square silver frame of her glasses finished me off. Of course I showed no hint of my erotic tumult as I spoke to this lovely woman, but when she strode to the front of Larry's clan to serve as their spokesperson, my pulse quickened.

A dozen of them showed up for our first meeting—aunts, uncles, parents, Virginia, and two other sisters. The grey-haired parents wept quietly, blotting their eyes with a handkerchief they passed back and forth between them. I was exhausted after a night on call. Given Larry's combat record, I had expected a disreputable mob, yet here was a clean and orderly gathering. They all rose when I entered the waiting room, looking at me with steady, intelligent eyes. After I explained Larry's guarded prognosis, Virginia sighed, wiped her eyes, asked three or four questions, and then thanked me by pressing my hand between her soft, warm palms.

Three days later, when I called to report that Larry was on his way to an emergency craniotomy, only Virginia, the parents, and one other sister showed up. They looked tired and somber as I went through my routine.

"To get at the blood clot on his brain," I explained, "we'll have to remove a piece of his skull. We can't be sure how much brain has been damaged, how much function he'll recover. There's a risk of paralysis, and after surgery you might notice a change in his personality."

The moment they heard "change in his personality," the whole group started. Their eyes, half-closed with fatigue an instant before, shot wide open. I paused. They all stared at me. I cleared my throat and was about to continue when Virginia grabbed both my arms.

"Doctor, Doctor—a change in personality? What do you mean?" She stood close, staring up at me, her eyes bright with desperation behind those square lenses.

"Well," I said, "it's like when we used to lobotomize schizophrenics and manic depressives. They changed, they calmed down; it seemed to work, but some had a bad outcome. Some became passive, detached, unkempt..."

"Doctor, listen to me," Virginia said, squeezing my arms. "How bad could it be? Doctor, if you only knew..." Tears streamed down her face. Her voice quavered. "You can't imagine what we've been through. Larry, my God, from the day he was born...it's been a nightmare. No one knows all the jails, the hospitals, the rehab wards. Can't you help us? 'Passive,' 'detached'—God, what a blessing! Anything would be better than..." Her voice trailed off. Her dark eyes remained fixed on mine.

My moment had come—a perfect moment. Here, in front of this desperate princess, I would show the poise and professional élan acquired during my years of medical training. In the lavatory a few minutes before, I had straightened my tie, combed my hair, and trimmed my bushy red beard with the scissors I carried in the pocket of my white coat. An opportunity like this couldn't be missed.

I missed it. How long did I stand there gaping, speechless, without a single useful thought in my brain? At last I stammered, "Gee...well, I don't know...I'll have to talk to Doctor Goldstein." I fled up the nearest flight of stairs, running so fast I tripped and almost cracked my head.

* * *

Larry Beaten lay supine on the OR table, covered head to toe by powder-blue surgical drapes. A beam of bright light shone down from an overhead fixture. In the center of the beam, beneath a hole in the drape, Larry's vermillion scalp lay naked to the world. Ron had shaved and scrubbed that scalp, painted it with Betadine, and was tracing the black curve of the impending incision with a sterile felt-tip pen. The room reeked of Betadine and isopropyl alcohol. Only a few hours remained before dawn. When I stepped up to the OR table, the scrub nurse at Ron's side pulled off her gloves and slung them into a trash bucket.

"I've got to go," she said. "They need me on another case."

As she disappeared through the *whoosh*ing pneumatic doors, the anesthesiologist looked up from the magazine in his lap. He yawned, grunted, cracked his knuckles, then lifted a clipboard from its hook on the side of the respirator and scribbled a note on the progress sheet to mark the time of the nurse's departure.

For the next hour, I handed instruments to Ron while he worked his way into Larry's brain. The flap of scalp—its thick, dark edges glistening with blood—curled back as the chrome spatula lifted it from the bone. The spatula made a soft scraping sound. Each time Ron cauterized the bleeding wound, the Bovie knife sparked and buzzed, giving off wisps of smoke that smelled like charred meat, until at last the flap lay coiled upon itself. Beneath the coil lay the clean white arc of the skull.

I slapped the handle of a drill into Ron's palm, then picked up a vacuum cannula to suck away the bony fragments. The bit made a steady crunching sound as it bore through Larry's skull. When it broke into the cranial cavity, the underlying dura matter bulged out through the hole, forming a dark, vein-laced blister that pulsed in sync with the respirator pumping air into Larry's lungs.

"Hey," Ron shouted to the anesthesiologist, who started and almost fell off his stool. "You'd better hyperventilate this guy right now. If we don't get his pressure down, his brain will come squirting out like toothpaste."

The anesthesiologist cleared his throat, muttered "OK, OK," then leaned forward to turn a dial on the respirator. The bellows in the respirator jumped to thirty cycles a minute. This lowered the carbon dioxide level in Larry's blood, leading to a physiologic cascade that reduced his intracranial pressure. After a few minutes, Ron said, "That's better, you can turn it down," but I wasn't convinced. To my fearful mind, the blister still seemed dangerously tense, ready to rupture and squirt brain paste all over the surgical drapes. Ron kept drilling. Soon four thumb-sized blisters formed the points of a square.

Next came the saw wire, an abrasive metal strand that Ron threaded beneath the skull from one hole to another. Using O-rings on the ends of the wire, he pulled back and forth until it sawed out through the bone, creating a linear cut, then set to work on the next pair of holes. When he sawed through the fourth side, the square of skull cracked loose and fell to the side. A fist-sized lump of brain bulged through the hole.

"There it is," Ron said.

Beneath the vein-laced surface of the lump lay a dark blotch. When Ron touched the blotch with his finger, it slithered about like an octopus. My knees wobbled. This was my first subdural hematoma, a blood clot trapped between the brain and the overlying dura matter. The texture of that glutinous slime made me gag, but I held my own until Ron thrust the vacuum cannula into the clot. Black tentacles oozed into the cannula, then surged in quivering jerks down the transparent vacuum tube. I gasped for breath. With each revolting quiver came an even more revolting sound: *slurp slurp slurp...sluurrp... sluuuuurrrrp...slurp slurp...sluuuuuuurrrrrrp.*

"Ron," I said, "I'm going to vomit."

"No, you're not," he said. "Gimme that retractor."

I gave him the retractor, swallowed the bile surging up the back of my throat, and blinked away the eye-stinging sweat that dripped down my forehead. In the end, I didn't vomit, but by the time I remembered Virginia's plea, Ron had finished cleaning up the mess. There before us, framed by the square hole in Larry's skull, lay what remained of his left frontal lobe—a tangle of fat grey worms laced with arteries and veins. Every trace of the clot was gone, its site marked by a shallow concavity.

"OK," Ron said, "time to close up."

"Uh, Ron," I said, "before you do that, we need to talk."

"About what?"

"How much of this guy's frontal lobe did he lose? Did we give him a lobotomy?"

"Oh, no," Ron said proudly. "He'll be right as rain. That clot just knocked off a bit of the left lobe, maybe

30 percent. And the right lobe, it's been shoved around a little, but it'll be fine. Tell his family everything's going to be OK."

It was time to unload. I described Virginia's bizarre plea, the eager murmur of approval from Larry's relatives when she urged me to do everything I could—and she meant *everything*—to change his personality.

"Ron," I said, "that family's great. The father's a professor at San Jose State, the sister's a peach and bright as hell. They've suffered the tortures of the damned since the day this S.O.B. was born. Did you see the scars on his face?"

"Yeah, yeah, yeah," Ron said. "I didn't count 'em, but I know his type."

"Well, do lobotomies work? All I know is what I read in books."

"Oh, yeah," Ron said, "lobotomies work just fine. I've lifted the hood on a lot of hoodlums—you know, chains, leather jackets, scars and tattoos everywhere—and when they lose enough frontal cortex, they wake up pretty nice guys. Sometimes they forget to bathe or brush their teeth, but they stop bashing people around."

"Well…" I said.

Ron and I looked at each other. A cap and mask covered everything except the eyes, but his eyes said it all. They gazed at me across the OR table, across the gaping skull of our unconscious patient. We stood in silence for a long time, sharing a dark, terrifying thought—a moral dilemma beyond anything I would encounter during the forty years of my medical career. Then Ron's gaze shifted to the anesthesiologist, who sat slumped in his chair, his cheek resting on an arm draped across the top of the respirator. His magazine lay on the floor. His breathing was noisy, slow, and rhythmic.

I knew what it would take—not much. Years before, I had watched my Uncle Melvin sauté a cow's brain. It was soft and squishy, oozing around the skillet like undercooked scrambled eggs. Just a few quick sucks— *slurp slurp slurp*—and the job would be finished.

* * *

Ron didn't finish the job. Later, he said it was the worst mistake of his life. We paid for that mistake when Larry Beaten woke from anesthesia with a hostile sneer on his lips, as though we had inflicted his injury rather than saved his life. We paid again during rounds every morning, when Larry—lying flat in bed, his head swathed in gauze—sneered and snarled and insulted without saying a word. With every encounter, hot blood rushed into Ron's face. And into mine. I loathed that jerk from the moment he opened his eyes.

"Sit up, dammit!" Ron said. "I'm talking to you!"

But for me, the most terrible price came when Virginia stormed out of her brother's room and caught me in the hallway. She grabbed the sleeve of my coat, her face contorted with pain and anger.

"My God, he's the same! Just the same!" Her dark eyes flashed behind those silver-wired glasses. Why, by what incomprehensible ethic, had we betrayed her, leaving her family in such torment?

Three months after his discharge, Larry paid the price himself when an ambulance again delivered his motionless body to Valley Medical Center. This time he was dead. His blood alcohol measured near the lethal range. He had run his car into a bridge abutment on the Junipero Serra Freeway, a hit so solid it froze the speedometer needle at 67 miles an hour. But Larry didn't die alone. The two young hitchhikers he had picked up a few minutes before the wreck sat huddled in the back seat. Admitted in coma to the neurosurgery ward, they both died within a few days.

* * *

Who killed those teenagers? Was it Larry Beaten. Was it Ron G.?

Doctors are not meant to play God. Surely they are not meant to commit crimes upon their patients. Unauthorized surgery is an assault, a felony of the highest order, but I wish—and I suspect Ron Goldstein wishes, even more fervently than I—that on this one occasion, in the dark of night, we had done the wrong thing.

CHAPTER ELEVEN

Death and the Maiden

Exhaustion clouds the mind. A forty-eight-hour shift turns the world into a waking dream, while sleep itself—in fragments snatched here and there on a lucky night—becomes a dreamless coma. A man begins to doubt his senses. At four a.m., why do all those around me—nurses, patients, fellow interns, janitors mopping linoleum floors with pine-scented detergent—look like cadavers, their faces gaunt and pocked with shadow? Why do my hands shake? Do I need to take a pill?

The old-timers assured me it used to be worse. On my neurosurgery rotation, the Admiral boasted that when he was an intern, nights off duty were rare and precious as diamonds.

"The word *intern*," he explained, "is derived from the French *interne*, 'to confine, as in a prison.' We worked round the clock, seven days a week. Half of us got a day off on Christmas and Easter, the other half on

Thanksgiving and New Year's Eve. Two days, plus a week's holiday a year—that was it."

The Admiral puffed on his charred meerschaum pipe, sending clouds of blue smoke drifting toward the ceiling of the hospital cafeteria. This pipe aroused controversy. Ron and I found it pleasant, redolent of cedar chips, but some of the nurses compared it to smoldering cow dung. The Admiral snatched the pipe from his mouth and gestured with the stem.

"Back then, they paid interns $50 a month. We slept four to a room in a stone barracks out behind the old San Francisco General. If you stayed on as a resident—not many did back then—you got a double. The chief resident had his own room and a private bath with one of those cast-iron tubs mounted on feet shaped like tiger claws. The damn thing must have been eight feet long."

The Admiral smiled and winked at me, glorying in my amazement. No doubt about it, I was mollycoddled—paid $837 a month, with two weeks of annual vacation and call every third night—while this old warrior had been on call almost every night of the year. Ron Goldstein had heard the Admiral's war stories before.

"But Admiral," he said, "how many times a night did they haul you out of bed for a code?"

"You know damn well—back then, we didn't have codes."

"What," I said, "your patients never arrested?"

"Don't be silly," the Admiral said. "Of course our patients died, but that was the end of it. Since there were no cardiac monitors, the nurses didn't know someone was dead until they came to take vital signs. By then, likely as not, they had gone stone cold. At morning rounds, we found an empty bed, and the head nurse made a discrete announcement—'Mister Jones has left us,' or something like that."

"Yeah," said Ron, "and what about IVs? How many times a night did they drag you out of bed to restart an infiltrated IV?"

The discussion proved enlightening. The institution of "house officer"—an intern or resident who worked, ate, and slept in a hospital twenty-four hours a day for months on end—arose at a time when cardiac arrests were shipped straight to the morgue and fluids were infused by hypodermoclysis, a subcutaneous needle any nurse could handle on her own. The troublesome gadgetry of modern medicine lay years in the future. Without the burden now imposed by respirators and defibrillators and endotracheal tubes, house officers worked hard all day, but at night they got plenty of sleep. Then—decade by decade, gadget by gadget—their nights turned into a frantic rush to pierce and pound and intubate what, back in the good old days, were considered warm corpses.

At lunch a few days later, the Admiral was puffing on his pipe and telling another war story when an angry shout filled the cafeteria.

"Jesus, man, I've been looking all over for you! Didn't you hear my page?"

Everyone in the cafeteria turned to look. A resident had discovered his intern slumped over, dead asleep, his head resting on folded arms. By his elbow lay an untouched sandwich and a cup of coffee. Mumbling, eyes glazed, tousled hair standing on end, the intern followed his resident out of the room. I noticed the sleeve of his white coat was wet with drool.

* * *

When my month on neurosurgery ended, I began my second ER rotation, but this time I copped the swing slot. Instead of six twelve-hour shifts, I would work two twelve-hour day shifts followed by three twelve-hour night shifts, an arrangement that gave my fellow interns their one day a week off. It sounded like paradise—only sixty hours a week, the cushiest job an intern could get except for the newborn nursery—but the assault on my biorhythm proved more brutal than I had expected. How does a man command himself to sleep in the sunshine Monday through Wednesday, then in the dark of night Thursday through Sunday? My house was six blocks from the hospital. Off duty on a summer afternoon, I stretched out on a lawn chair in my backyard, looking up through the leaves of three acacia trees and listening to ambulance sirens while I struggled to sleep. *Struggle*—not a good word when it comes to sleep.

The sirens rose out of the distance, faint at first, pulsing up and down against a hazy summer sky. Jangled nerves. No sleep. On my nights off duty, evenings brought more sirens, an endless procession that wailed off and on until dawn. I ground my teeth, tossed in bed, counted my pulse into the thousands trying to calm my racing mind. I paced in circles, read medical journals, and stared out a window at the darkness. No sleep. When at last I lay in bed, drifting down toward slumber, I hovered half asleep and half awake, a fraction from blessed oblivion, until a flash of anxiety exploded in my brain, jolting my limbs with electrical shocks. All hope of sleep was lost.

This wasn't a relapse of my hypochondria but a devastating combination of insomnia and panic attacks. A man needs courage to tap a spine or thrust a trocar into a swollen abdomen, and courage, I soon discovered, leaks out through the cracks of an exhausted mind. *How long before I miss a terminal arrhythmia or prescribe a fatal dose of coumadin?* I thought. Every time I thrust a subclavian needle beneath a patient's collarbone, my mind's eye saw the sharp tip ripping a hole in his innominate artery.

An intern sent an eighty-year-old preacher home from the ER with a prescription for gas pains, but while the old man waited in line at a drugstore to fill the prescription, he keeled over from a ruptured abdominal aneurysm. The scandal raced through the Valley Medical Center. After that, in my sleepless, feverish brain, every wailing ambulance carried a dead patient I had sent home from the ER a few hours before.

Ellen Stevens was the ER director, a kind mentor and a skillful physician, but she called interns into her office for a chat if their hands shook and they ordered too many consults because they feared killing someone.

"What's wrong, John? You did fine when you worked here last summer, but you don't seem to be your old self. Maybe you should have a talk with Gallagher."

Sam Gallagher, the director of the mental-health clinic. He had grey eyes and a solemn, avuncular voice. His curly white hair always needed a trim, but he was a good man. He didn't make me feel like a freak.

"It's OK," he told me. "You'd be surprised how many docs have the same problem. We've got to get you some sleep. Here, take one of these four times a day."

An hour after my first dose of Librium, a siren became just another noise. I slept soundly and woke slowly, gazing through acacia leaves at fragments of a purpling sky. Languor settled in, a lovely indifference, but...where was the bouquet of honeysuckle that once drifted across my yard on the afternoon breeze? A steaming hot bath didn't bring its usual pleasure, nor did the pastrami sandwich I ate for supper or a glimpse of my wife as she stepped from the shower. To her relief, alas, that pale and perfect nakedness had lost its power over me. My libido vanished. *Oh, well,* I thought, *the price to pay; no molecule is smart enough to block the pain and let the pleasure pass.*

* * *

By the grace of Librium, I survived my ER rotation, but the reprieve was short-lived. On my next rotation, the medicine service, rounds began at six a.m. From the waning darkness of early dawn, I slogged my way through a ward full of bad livers, bad lungs, and bad bowels. Nor was that the end of my labors. Every Tuesday and Thursday afternoon, no matter how much hell broke loose on the ward, I had to staff the General Medical Clinic. GMC—a refuge for the ancient, the decrepit, the lost of the earth, shipped in by the dozen from nursing homes all over Santa Clara County. When the time came, I was always rushing about to get my ward patients under control. Infiltrated IVs, stat blood gases, leaky chest tubes—all conspired to make me late.

The operator paged me through the overhead speakers: "Doctor Gamel, urgent to GMC," repeating the message in ever more strident tones as the minutes passed. At last I rushed down to the GMC gauntlet, a hallway filled with mummies, their wheelchairs lined hub to hub as far as the eye could see. I walked fast, lest one not blinded by age should recognize me, call my name, reach out a quavering hand to grab my sleeve. In the heat of summer, their upraised arms were bare, their liver-spotted flesh hanging in folds. On a bad day, Mr. Eakins sat near the entrance. His vision had been restored by cataract surgery. Behind thick lenses, his huge eyes caught sight of me. He reached out to grasp my arm. He called, "Doctor Gamel." The word spread down the line: "Doctor Gamel...Doctor Gamel...Doctor Gamel..."

Their voices called my name, but their eyes said so much more: *Oh Doctor, please stop and chat. I've not been out of my nursing home since our last visit three months ago, and it would be such a lovely thing if you could stand beside me for a moment. Smile down at me. Take my hand. You would do this, Doctor, surely you would do this if you knew how long it's been since anyone touched me.*

But I was late, always late. Arriving at last, I ran back and forth between two cubicles as nurses shuttled patients in and out with the cruel rhythm of a metronome. Hurry hurry hurry. The instant I entered a cubicle, the wheelchair-bound soul began her lamentations: phlegm, gas pains, shortness of breath, a roommate who spat on the floor and sucked her teeth all night.

I said, "Oh, my…sorry to hear that…you poor thing…" as I peered into their eyes, their noses, their throats, percussed and auscultated their chests, then scribbled prescriptions and chart notes. Finally came that awful moment.

No, no, Doctor, not yet. They said it with their eyes. *Please, Doctor, can't you give me just a little more…a little more…?*

Time—the currency of life?

More time? No, I can't.

* * *

The innocents among us see death as an event rather than a process. Sometimes it works that way. A bullnecked handball player clutches his chest and falls face-down, breaking his nose on the hardwood floor. Perhaps he's the lucky one, a DOA rushed to the ER on a slow afternoon, his T-shirt damp with sweat and his arteries pulseless as a stone. Five o'clock shadow darkens his jowls. Not much blood from the broken nose, just two streaks drying on his upper lip.

But for most of us, death comes in tiny slices. We rot slowly, our tissues withering year by year, leaving only wrinkles and decrepitude and—for my GMC patients—a loneliness cruel and parching as the desert sun. I touched those lonely people, gave them hugs and pats on the knee, but every instant I felt time's hot breath on my neck. Five-thirty. Six o'clock. My God, what's happening up on the ward? I imagine my resident—frantic, hollow-eyed, rushing from disaster to disaster and cursing my absence.

Finally, after weeks of GMC torment, the bottom dropped out of my world. Up on the medical ward, two alcoholics were hemorrhaging from their esophageal varices. An overdose of potassium sent a patient into ventricular fibrillation. The page operator began calling me at one-fifteen, her voice blaring through the overhead speakers, but it was almost two o'clock when I made my way down to the GMC inferno, where a nurse found a bloodstain on the tail of my white coat and sent me back upstairs to change.

The first patient was scrawny as a stick, an ancient, cheerful nun with dyed blue hair. She lifted my spirits, but her garrulous, sleeve-plucking affection put me further behind. My next two patients were demented, one of them in the terminal stages of a brain tumor. Their filmy eyes and corpse-grey faces sent me over the edge.

Three days before, hoping to escape my peaceful prison, I had stopped taking Librium, and now the price of my foolish courage was upon me—a panic attack. My hands trembled. Sweat poured down my face and soaked the collar of my white shirt. I rushed to the lavatory to swallow a Librium, but an hour would elapse before the philter could work its magic, and in the meantime I had to keep up the rhythm: force a smile; choke out my words through a raw, tight throat; examine the patient; scribble notes with a trembling hand; announce my farewell; then rush to the next cubicle, where another desperate mummy awaited my healing touch.

Then all was lost. There sat the patient, but where was the wheelchair? And my God—the patient! I saw glossy dark hair hanging down to her shoulders. I saw a sleeveless aqua minidress, a golden expanse of bare arms and legs. Audrey Hepburn? No, not quite, a little too broad in the face. And overdone. She wore pancake makeup, heavy eye shadow, lashes matted with mascara—a painted doll redolent of lilac and musk. Some miracle, a warp in the space-time continuum, had transported a *Vogue* model into my cubicle.

"Hello," she said, smiling. "My name's Linda Baker."

Linda had perfect white teeth and full, red lips. There was elegance in the angle of her crossed legs, the poise of her thin, squared shoulders, her hands folded modestly in her lap. Had I lost my mind? Was this a hallucination? The young, the rich, the beautiful—they never came anywhere near the General Medical Clinic, yet here was a sylph dressed like a fashion plate. At last I spoke.

"What…uh…brings you here today?"

"My face," she said.

"Your face?"

"Yes. It gets numb. Sometimes. Numb and a little tingly."

"When does this happen?"

"Oh, sometimes…sometimes…at dinner…"

Her face remained calm, but she began wringing her hands.

"Do you have any other symptoms?" I asked.

"Oh, yes," she gasped. "I get light-headed. Things spin around like I'm going to faint. My heart thumps so hard I can feel it beating inside my head." She squeezed her eyes shut and pressed her fingers to her temples. Her lips trembled. "I just...can't...sleep."

Linda blotted her eyes. Streaks of mascara crept down her cheeks. The tissues I handed her collapsed one by one into soggy wads. My own panic had begun to wane. Perhaps I wasn't insane, but what was this creature doing in GMC?

"It sounds to me as if you're under a lot of stress," I said.

"Stress? Oh, certainly not. I'm fine. Just fine. Got married two months ago."

She sniffed, smiled, blew her nose, and then held up her left hand to show the diamond ring and matching circlet. A small diamond, less beautiful than the slender, honey-gold hand it adorned. I struggled to clear my mind, focus on her problem. My voice was hoarse but remained loud and full of authority. Surely she had a clue, I insisted, some hint of where this panic monster was coming from?

"No," she said, raising her chin. "You should send me to a brain surgeon. I think I've got a tumor."

I was running late, desperately late. The clinic nurse had twice cracked the door of the cubicle to give me a glowering rebuke. Again, panic came upon me—what to do with this peculiar girl? I had long since mastered the subtleties of hemorrhoids and emphysema and congestive heart failure, but this was a new game, and that lovely, expectant face left me stupefied.

Ah, I remembered at last—this was not a new game for me, and what was good for the doctor might be good for the patient. I didn't have the time or training to sort through Linda's psyche, but perhaps Librium might work the same magic for her it had for me. Once her anxieties were quelled, the poor girl might sort out her own problems.

My plan worked. Almost. Linda missed her follow-up appointment, but a week later, the pharmacy called to report that she wanted more Librium. "Absolutely not," I said. "Tell her that if she wants more, she'll have to see me in clinic."

When she returned, her hair was bobbed, and she wore a black silk dress that came below the knee. The mascara and pancake makeup had been restored. My houri was her old self, fetching and poised as ever, but this time she remained dry-eyed throughout the interview. Her tingling and numbness had vanished. She slept soundly, her nerves calm as a glassy pool. Well, yes, a faint mist seemed to float in front of her eyes, and sometimes she saw halos around peoples' heads, but that didn't bother her. Nothing bothered her.

But the stress, the terrible anxiety attacks she had suffered—what was all that about? The topic didn't interest her. She sighed, grimaced, and said, "What's the point of talking about all that stuff?" She said it three times, but I persisted, until finally the story came out.

Linda was seventeen, the only child of a wealthy lawyer who had been widowed since her birth. She was also a high school dropout, married to a twenty-eight-year-old pothead who watched TV all day and couldn't find a job. Linda's father, a closet alcoholic, had forbidden the marriage, and her defiance had provoked an outrage that only grew worse when she turned off the burglar alarm in their Los Altos Hills home so her new husband could haul away two trunks filled with her designer clothes. After that, the father refused to give her a cent. She was in the GMC because her health-insurance card had expired; when she returned home to ask her father for a new card, he caught sight of her coming up the sidewalk and pitched two andirons through the living-room window.

Now Linda and her husband lived on welfare in a hovel they shared with his family in a seedy section of San Jose. What kind of people were they? Well, they threw food at each other across the dinner table. When Linda refused to eat her mother-in-law's boiled turnip greens, the woman screamed obscenities and dumped the plate on the floor. The two sisters-in-law pulled Linda's hair—not in jest, but with vicious jerks that raised knots on her scalp. She parted her hair to show me a wheal the size of my thumb.

A stressful life indeed. After Linda finished her story, we sat in silence for a long time. My judgment was clouded by pride—no doubt she wanted to thank me. I waited for grateful tears, a gush of praise, perhaps a warm embrace for the clever regimen that had calmed her anxieties and allowed her to sort out her life. But her face…that expression…what was it? Sitting with her back straight, one arm akimbo, half turned in her chair, Linda kept staring at me.

Was she expectant? Angry? Something had gone wrong. The stern face melted into a smile. The black dress ascended, revealing a golden expanse of thigh. After several moments of a silent, come-hither gaze, the slippery black hem inched higher still. Her legs were flawless—long, smooth, and tanned—but my dead libido saved the day. Her exposed thighs didn't arouse me. They alarmed me. What did this strange woman want?

"I need more Librium," Linda said.

"More Librium? But…no, you need to do something about your life, get away from that awful place, those terrible people you live with."

"Do what? I have no money, nowhere to go. Besides, the medicine you gave me—that's great stuff. I can live with anybody, long as I can get some sleep and keep my nerves from tearing me to pieces."

A horrifying proposition: Linda wanted me to cast her in a perpetual Librium trance so she could endure her misery. She read the shock in my face. Her smile vanished. Now she was rigid, defiant, her chin uplifted.

"You started it, Doctor. You gave me the pills."

"But your father…you could ask him for help…"

Her eyes blazed. The pancake makeup cracked into ugly furrows across her brow. She snarled, "Why that… that miserable bastard! I'd rather rot in hell!"

* * *

I never saw Linda again. No doubt she soon got all the happy pills she wanted from other doctors. Perhaps to this day, the poor woman sleeps soundly in her house of numbness, and if she does, she's not alone. The summer after my freshman year of college, I worked as a file clerk at Ford Motor Company's distribution hub in Doraville, Georgia, a northern suburb of Atlanta. In a cinderblock shed dreary as a tomb, surrounded by acres of tarmac and 2,000 Ford Fairlanes, my stout, red-nosed boss began each day with a sight gag. He slammed the door behind him, filled a paper cup from the water cooler, announced, "Seven years, four months, two days"—the time left before his retirement—then tossed a Miltown capsule into the air and caught it in his mouth.

Miltown was the tranquilizer of choice. Years later, Roche Pharmaceuticals discovered Librium, which dominated the sedative market until displaced by Valium, the ultimate happy pill. Within a decade, millions of men and women the world over were grazing their way through life like so many contented cows.

When my GMC houri appeared, I was hooked on happy pills myself. It would make a good story if her pharmaceutical seduction had given me an epiphany; if, in a flash of insight, I had thrown my Librium into the trash. It didn't happen that way. For years, I never left home without a hand-carved ivory pillbox tucked in my pocket. Yes, like many of my fellow physicians, I was a tranquilizer freak, but I stood above the hoi polloi by carrying my pills in an artistic receptacle. I never overdosed, always kept away from hard drugs, and stayed alert and bright-eyed. Like opposing electrical charges, my anxieties neutralized the soporific molecules flowing through my bloodstream, allowing my competence to remain unimpaired. But my memory of Linda—her craving for oblivion, her hard, desperate eyes—worked on me, even as I took Librium, then Valium, with the faithfulness of a diabetic taking his insulin.

Such reliable, magical medicine. Take one now and peace will descend. Take one now and nothing—your mistaken diagnoses, your heartbroken patients, even your cold, unhappy wife—will disturb you in the least.

And yet, despite their magical powers, I gave up happy pills. It was not a sudden decision, nor inspired by a soul-searching effort. No, my salvation came from images. During my months in the GMC, I saw the withered faces of men and women nearing the end of their mortal tether. Those faces stayed with me. They wandered through my dreams, through my waking thoughts, and over the years they taught me this: only a man who lives forever can afford to squander his days in a joyless stupor.

Death comes to most of us in tiny slices, but in the end, I decided it would be best not to cut those slices with my own hand.

CHAPTER TWELVE

The Dark Mirror

Death can be viewed from many angles: I die, you die, he-she-it dies; we die, you die, they die.

Death is the ultimate disconnect, yet it tells us much about our living selves, serving as a dark mirror that reflects the truths obscured by our vitality.

Chance, risk, fate—what do they mean to you? What do they mean to me?

One of my cardiology patients needed open-heart surgery for severe aortic stenosis and mitral insufficiency, a procedure that, back in the 1970s, carried a mortality of 30 percent. When an orderly came to wheel him away for what might spell his doom, the patient wouldn't budge, clinging to the bedrails and resisting every plea for fifteen minutes so he could finish watching the latest episode of *As the World Turns*. The moment it was over, he thanked the orderly for waiting and climbed onto the gurney.

Should we flee from death or rush to embrace him before he reaches our door? The annals of ophthalmology record a case of what one might call anticipatory suicide. An archeologist in her early sixties, healthy except for a mastectomy five years before, attributed the visual loss in her right eye to a recurrence of her breast cancer. In a fit of despair, she and her husband took overdoses of Phenobarbital. An autopsy showed that her blurred vision was due to optic neuropathy, a localized inflammation of the optic nerve. There was no sign of malignancy anywhere in her body.

Audie Murphy was fifteen years old when America entered World War II. At 5'5" and 110 pounds, he had the physique, the voice, and the cherubic face of a choir boy, yet during numerous assaults through withering enemy fire, he killed 240 German soldiers. On one occasion, he stole behind the lines, seized a Nazi machine gun, then wiped out a whole squad. By expert reckoning, the most dangerous of these assaults carried a risk of mortality greater than 90 percent.

I had to face down my own fear of death. At the height of my flying phobia, a table published by the Federal Aviation Administration informed me that each commercial flight caries a risk of one in 1.73 million, a fact so reassuring I needed only ten milligrams of Valium to get on an airplane and one martini an hour to stay on it without keeling over in a dead faint. I always packed four or five Beefeater miniatures in my carry-on bag in case the pilot cancelled beverage service because of rough weather.

Audie Murphy survived World War II and won thirty-three medals for bravery. In 1971, at the age of forty-four, he died in a plane crash.

If death is the eternal footman, should we give him a tip? During a PBS special on the life of Vladimir Horowitz, the narrator interviewed Wanda Toscanini Horowitz, Vladimir's widow and the great conductor's daughter. She spoke fondly of the overstuffed chair in which she sat during the interview. In that chair, at the age of eighty-five, with all his faculties intact, Vladimir had suffered a quiet and painless death.

"My friends call me strange for keeping it around," she said. "They insist I should get rid of it, but this chair is my favorite thing in all the world. I sit here often, especially in the evening."

* * *

Maggie Mae Smith, a tiny, vigorous, rawboned woman in her late eighties, came to the orthopedic ward at Valley Medical Center with a broken hip. I found her pleasant enough, but the nursing staff lost their hearts to the old lady. She was all smiles and compliments, grateful for every kindness. Never in her life had she allowed anyone to wait on her. A delightful but difficult patient, she never pushed her call button, wept with vexation when she had to request a bedpan from a passing aide, and heaped thanks on the technician who drew her blood. The morning after her admission, I saw one of the aides tying ribbons in the remaining wisps of Maggie's snow-white hair. The charge nurse, frowning with anxiety, grilled the ortho resident.

"Doctor, Maggie's surgery—how does it look?"

It didn't look good. The broken hip was bad—a technical challenge, soft and chalky from osteoporosis—

but her heart was the real problem. She had ventricular hypertrophy, congestive failure, atrial fibrillation with runs of ventricular tachycardia. The anesthesia resident took one look at the EKG and called the chief of anesthesia down to examine Maggie himself. He threw a fit. General anesthesia was out of the question.

That news sent Aaron Mason, the orthopedic attending, into a fit of his own. He had never done a hip replacement under local anesthesia. A 6'6" bench-warmer on the UCLA basketball team during his college years, he was proud, stuffy, and—according to the ortho resident—a fair to middling surgeon. He had curly blonde hair. Behind his back, while he scrubbed his huge hands at the OR sink, the nurses giggled and rolled their eyes and said, "Ohhh, here comes Doctor Goldilocks." He laughed often, raucously, but it was the laugh of a man whose heart is filled with dust. His arrogance almost got his ass kicked by Maggie Smith's son, a sturdy fellow whose bald head hovered an inch or two below Mason's red bowtie.

"Mr. Smith," Mason said, "you need to understand that if we operate, your mother might not survive the surgery." His voice was loud. I suspect he was afraid Maggie might blemish his record by dying under the knife, but he came across as impatient and patronizing. "I want to do the best for her, but in this case, perhaps the best thing is to leave her alone."

Smith said, "Jesus Christ," then turned on his heel and strode out of the conference room. He paused in front of a row of vending machines across the hall. Through the doorway, Mason and the resident and I watched his back as he studied multicolored bags of Doritos, Cheez Whiz, Lay's Potato Chips. He didn't buy anything, but after what seemed a long time, he strode back into the room and stood before Aaron, rocking on his heels, tilting his head back to look into that handsome, startled face.

"Doctor Mason," Smith said, "I'm not an idiot." There was a quaver in his voice that spoke not of tears but of an iron will. His eyes bulged with anger. Mason backed up a step. Smith followed him. "Of course my mother may die," he said. "She's eighty-nine years old. But if you don't operate, she'll be an invalid the rest of her life, and for her that would be ten times worse than death. Why don't you stick to the bones and let my mother and me worry about the rest?"

The next day, we operated under spinal anesthesia. Maggie didn't turn a hair. She lay on the OR table wide awake, a frail, copper-skinned doll in a gauze mask and powder-blue surgical cap. We turned her on her side for the spinal injection, tucking knees to chin until her bony spine and ribs curved like the markings on a conch shell. The only sound she made was a soft grunt when the needle popped through her dura matter. Within moments, she was numb from the waist down. I scrubbed her naked hip with Phisohex, stained it with Betadine, then helped a nurse lay on surgical drapes until all that showed of Maggie's torso was a maroon-colored square of sterile flesh.

During these maneuvers, Maggie gazed around the OR like an awestruck child. "This is such a wonderful place," she said. "I've never seen anything like it in my life."

Three hours later, Maggie lay in the recovery room with her femur pinned and the wound on her lean brown hip sewn tight. Her vital signs remained stable. By dinnertime, she was back in her room.

Later that evening, the ward clerk interrupted my rounds to give me a message: "The Smith family wants to talk to you."

I've gone over that sentence again and again in my mind, and of this I am certain: nothing the clerk said, neither her words nor the tone of her voice, carried a hint of urgency. Yes, I am certain—"The Smith family wants to talk to you." That was all.

After rounds, I treated a wound infection, then changed several dressings. Finally I washed my hands and went to Maggie's room. She lay alone, her thin arms resting by her side. She was dead. When I put my hand on her forehead, it felt cool. Her eyes were half-closed. The exposed corneas had begun to cloud over with the ground-glass haze of dehydration.

I called the son to tell him his mother had died.

"Yes, I know," he said. His voice was full of grief, a dry, unbroken grief, weighted with sorrow beyond words. There was no quaver, no sobbing, just exhaustion and heartache.

"You...you already knew?" I said. A surge of guilt twisted my tongue. "I'm sorry...didn't know...the clerk, she didn't say...rounds went on...I got there quick as..."

Smith waited until I stammered into silence.

"We were all there," he said. "We were talking to mother, and she just faded away. At first we panicked, my son Jamie ran out, said something to a clerk about getting a doctor, then we looked at each other. We waited. Nobody came. It was a blessing."

"You...you didn't stay?" I asked.

"Jamie said for sure you guys would be pounding on her chest. You had to; it was part of the rules, no matter how long she'd been dead. He said you might break her ribs. We didn't want to see someone pounding on our mother. We waited ten or fifteen minutes. Everybody kissed her, then we left."

"But...why?" I asked. "Didn't you know...we might have revived her..." Even as this nonsense dribbled out of my mouth, I choked on my stupidity. Or duplicity. What kind of a world do doctors live in?

Maggie's son was on me in an instant.

"And tell me, Doctor, what happens when you stomp the life back into an eighty-nine-year-old woman?" Now his voice quavered but with anger, not sorrow. "What's left lying there in that bed after you break all her ribs?"

The son was a forgiving fellow. Of course he was right—our chances of bringing his mother back from the grave as anything other than a vegetable or a hopeless cripple were less than one in a thousand. Perhaps he sensed the remorse in my voice or felt sorry for the fool I had made of myself. I don't remember what I said, but somehow, with brazen persistence, I asked permission for an autopsy. Our chief of staff reminded us at morbidity and mortality rounds that if we don't know why the patient died, we'll never get any smarter. Maggie's son interrupted my wheedling, semicoherent pleas.

"Yes, Doctor, you have my permission for an autopsy. If…if you think it will help. Mother would have wanted it that way."

The son was wrong about one thing. By the time I arrived, Maggie's body had grown cool, and I talked my colleagues out of pounding on her chest, but I didn't tell him that. I did call him a week later with the autopsy results: brittle plaques filled Maggie's coronary arteries and choked off her aorta, leaving her heart a sea of infarcts. Only a few tenuous collaterals fed the surviving myocardium. The woman had a dozen good reasons to die. For years, perhaps a decade, she had lived on borrowed time.

* * *

Then there was Elmer Smith. Yes, Smith—a small but striking irony. Measured by the scale of human worth, this poor man lived on the opposite side of the universe from Maggie Mae. He almost won me the *Q*-sign trophy, an unofficial award given each month to the intern with the most dehydrated living patient. *Q*-sign refers to an open mouth with a tongue drooping out one corner, the classic presentation when a patient's serum sodium rises so high from loss of fluids it puts him into a coma. Elmer's value, 203 milli-equivalents per liter, would kill a camel, but that same month a rival intern beat me with a boozer who had passed out in his sauna and boiled his sodium up to 217 before someone found him.

When they rolled Elmer in from the ER, he was hanging by a thread. His nursing-home chart told a dismal story: Wernicke-Korsakoff syndrome, the medical term for alcohol-induced brain rot, had left him in a vegetative stupor. After eight years in the nursing home, pneumonia plus a summer heat wave and a failure of the home's air-conditioning had turned his body into a pillar of salt. According to a long note written by a social worker, he was born in Australia, emigrated to California in his thirties, served as Tiburon's mayor, and ran a Mercedes dealership. Elmer remained a respected citizen until one fateful Sunday morning when he showed up for mass at the Holy Saints Church wearing tennis shorts and a pair of sandals. He was disoriented, babbling, and—a bad sign— stone-cold sober. The neurologists at Pacific Medical Center gave Elmer their best, but by that time the booze had dissolved too much grey matter.

With his wasted torso and age-darkened skin, Elmer resembled nothing so much as a rusty railroad spike. His head was a skull. His crusted lips formed a perfect *O*, while his tongue, dry as a cinder, was stuck to the corner of his mouth. His pulse and respirations were barely detectable.

Fitzy, my resident on the medicine service, washed his hands of the case.

"He's all yours, Gamel. Just don't do anything heroic. You'd better get hold of his family and hang some crepe."

Only one signature appeared on the sign-in sheet taped to the front of Elmer's nursing-home chart—Mrs. Eleanor Smith Huber. At first, her visits came every week, then, for a while, every month. Five years had passed since the last visit.

Eleanor Huber wore a green silk dress, matching high-heeled shoes, and three strings of pearls. Amidst the grey walls and coffee-colored linoleum of Valley Medical's charity ward, she shone like an emerald. She was tall and spoke with a cultured Australian accent, but in her subdued, down-gazing face I saw the hint of ancient violence: a backlit figure lurching through a doorway, the shouts and slaps of nightly rages.

"Is he..." she said, but her voice broke off. She clutched a small black purse to her chest and stared at the floor. She blinked away tears.

"It doesn't look good," I said. "He has pneumonia in both lungs, and his body is terribly dehydrated."

"What are his chances?"

"His chances? Well..." This was an intelligent woman, I thought—surely she could see that after eight years in a vegetative coma, her father's time had come. "To be honest, we don't expect him to live."

Her head snapped back. For the first time, her eyes met mine. She frowned and wiped a tear from her cheek with the back of her hand.

"If he's that sick, then why don't you put him in the intensive care unit?"

"The intensive care unit? Well...he's very sick, but... his mind...he's been gone for years. We hadn't planned to use aggressive therapy."

"Doctor!" she gasped, glowering at me. Her face darkened. "Why that's...that's murder."

When I reported this conversation to Fitzy, he covered our tracks by ordering the nurses to put a daily dose of Penicillin down Elmer's nasogastric tube. It didn't cure his pneumonia. We never saw his daughter again.

* * *

Maggie Mae and Elmer taught me the subtleties of death. When love runs deep, when the heart remains bound and unconflicted, death is not the enemy. The agony suffered by Elmer's daughter came not from his lingering departure but from his tragic life. Yet this was abstract knowledge, a philosophical insight that seemed far removed from my own life, while Bryan Cubbage's death gave me a personal torment unlike anything I have ever known. He was a harmless old veteran by the time I met him. Emerging unscathed from the Battle of the Bulge and three assaults on the Siegfried Line, he had acquired a dozen tattoos, needle tracks down both arms, and a knife scar from his umbilicus to his sternum.

"They cut me good," he said. "I was a stupid shit, paid for a bag of horse with a phony hundred. They should've killed me."

Now a loose-skinned man in his fifties, blowzy and disheveled, he attended AA meetings every week and lived a quiet life. Eczema had given his skin a frosty patina of scales. His stringy hair was flaked with dandruff. Radiation therapy for squamous carcinoma of a tonsil had marked his left neck and jaw with a red patch the size of a saucer. The radiation plus three courses of chemotherapy had dropped his white count to a dangerous level, but he felt well and ate well, spending hours a day watching television or trading war stories with his fellow veterans in the hospital lobby.

Amid the dilapidation of Bryan's person, there lurked one precious item. This slothful man, a sartorial and hygienic calamity, was obsessed with time and with the jewel-bright instruments that measure its passing. On his wrist he wore a Bulova Accutron. I had read about this gem in *Popular Mechanics*. It costs hundreds of dollars. An advertisement in the *New Yorker* showed a gorgeous man, clean-favored and imperially slim, his wrist aglitter with an Accutron. Bryan's Accutron was solid gold, eighteen karat, its second hand turning not in jerks but smooth as butter, smooth as the turning of the earth itself.

"Come on, Doc," he said one evening. "I've got something to show you."

He led me to his room, where we listened to a broadcast from a shortwave radio on his bedside table. We stood with our heads so close I could smell the musty odor of his unwashed hair. First we heard only the rhythmic ticks of a metronome marking one-second intervals, but then, after a few seconds, a mechanical voice droned, "At the tone, the time will be twenty-two-fifty-two Greenwich Mean Time...*tick...tick...tick... tick...beep!*" I felt a thrill when the second hand of Bryan's Accutron fell dead on the money.

A week later, I was down the hall helping Fitzy intubate a comatose cirrhotic when Bryan suffered his first cardiac arrest. Someone called a code over the intercom, and within seconds a crush of doctors and nurses exploded into the room. Scrub suits, white caps, IV poles waving about, a respiratory tech clattering down the hall with a crash cart trailing hoses and extension cords.

"Gimme that scope!"

"Where's the endo tube?"

"Bicarb, dammit!"

"Epi, where's the epi?"

"I've got the paddles, gimme some paste...OK, stand back."

It worked. A few seconds after the defibrillator sent a spine-arching jolt through Bryan's body, the EKG monitor showed sinus rhythm. Minutes later, he moved his arms, turned his head, and stared wide-eyed at the circle of faces around his bed. He gestured for someone to take the endo tube out of his trachea. His blood pressure measured 90/60, pretty good for a man minutes away from cardiac arrest, so Fitzy pulled the tube, but he should have known better. Considering the IV fluids and the blast of epinephrine we had pumped into Bryan, the pressure should have been higher. Three days later, when the blood cultures grew out E. coli, we realized all had been lost from the first moment. Bryan had a florid Gram-negative infection.

Soon after the first arrest, he coded again. I was there. His eyes closed and he stopped breathing. The cardiac monitor showed ventricular fibrillation. The doctors and nurses rushed back. For half an hour, they prodded and cajoled his infected body, but this time he stayed dead. His sphincters loosened. The fecal smell of death filled the room.

The admitting clerk had marked the front of Bryan's chart in bold red letters: *CATHOLIC*. With Catholics, we always left the respirator going until a priest had delivered last rites.

The priest showed up after midnight. His eyes were glazed with sleep behind gold-rimmed spectacles, but he wore immaculate vestments, and his iron-grey hair gleamed with pomade. His pomade or aftershave smelled like lemons. I hoped he would not suspect the truth, hoped the rhythmic *hiss...clunk...hiss...clunk...hiss... clunk* of the respirator would give the illusion of life, but the instant the priest's hand touched Bryan's face, he looked at me. Was that a conspiratorial glint in his eye or a resentful glint? Last rites are meant to be given in the waning moments of life, yet Bryan was already cool. We had called the poor man out of bed to bless a corpse.

"Hail Mary, full of grace, the Lord is with thee; blessed art thou among women..." His reedy voice, vaguely effeminate, wove its way through the mechanical breaths of the respirator. As the priest chanted—touching Bryan's eyes, ears, nose, lips, and hands—he kept glancing at me. Did he suspect what was in my heart?

The priest left. The bouquet of lemons faded from the room. It was one o'clock in the morning. At last, Bryan and I were alone. I unplugged the respirator. The rhythmic sounds of false life ceased, filling the room, the hallway—the entire hospital—with a silence so profound I could hear a footstep a hundred feet away.

Bryan Cubbage—dilapidated and friendless. Bryan Cubbage—the faithless lover of many women, the named father of three children, the unnamed father of who knows how many more. Decades had passed since a relative last spoke to him. No one in the world would know or care that his body lay motionless, consumed by the final agony, descending into the chill that knows no end with a treasure strapped to one icy wrist.

It was a terrible moment. I meant to walk out of the room, but I had to sit down. I sat on a chair next to

Bryan's bed and leaned my head against the mattress. I took long, slow breaths. My soul was beyond thievery—yes, well beyond, sick to the point of nausea. In the end I did the right thing, but Bryan's death told me more about myself than I wanted to know.

CHAPTER THIRTEEN

The Funnel

E dward Brown was born on a bad night—bad for him, bad for me, and bad for Ames Miller, the resident in charge of my pediatric team. Neither Ames nor I were destined for a minute's sleep, nor would we sit down, even once, for any purpose other than scribbling notes in dozens of charts as we trotted around Valley Medical Center under summons from the page operator. Despite the tinny acoustics of the overhead speakers, she sounded fetching—throaty, a bit breathless, with a lilting note at the end of each phrase: "Doctor Miller, STAT to the ER...Doctor Miller, STAT to peds 1A...Doctor Miller...Doctor Miller..." It strikes me as poignant that I heard her voice throughout the year of my internship, all the while fantasizing a lovely young woman, yet I never saw her face.

It was April, a warm early spring, and by midnight the ER had plagued my team with three ersatz cases of meningitis. The real problem was a squirrelly ER intern who didn't know how to test a child for the symptoms of meningeal irritation. Every time a feverish toddler refused to turn his head to look at a set of jiggling keys, the intern diagnosed a stiff neck, and another "Doctor Miller, STAT to the ER" came over the PA system. Ames finally dragged the intern into the cast room and slammed the door.

"Goddamn it, man," he shouted, "give the kid at least ten seconds. Time it with your watch. And try a rattle or a squeaky toy. A sick kid doesn't give a shit for a bunch of keys, no matter how loud you jiggle them."

At two a.m., a preemie on a respirator spit out his endotracheal tube. The reinsertion was too tricky for Ames. He made a couple of tries, then spent fifteen minutes coaxing an anesthesia resident out of the OR. By the time they got the tube threaded past the epiglottis and into the soft, pencil-sized trachea, the infant's face was pitch black, but he pinked up right away, then delighted the nurses with a convulsive bowel movement. Minutes later, while Ames and I were on the peds ward restarting infiltrated IVs, we got paged back to the ER to see an eight-year-old boy who had been poked in the eye with a lighted cigarette. The ophthalmology resident took care of the corneal burn, but Ames had to haggle with a social worker over whether the kid's father should be charged with child abuse. I ran back up to work on the IVs, but ten minutes later Ames called me on the ward phone.

"For God's sake, Gamel, I'm trying to keep this poor bastard out of jail, but OB won't leave me alone. The charge nurse keeps babbling about some newborn with his guts falling out. Get up there and see what's going on."

* * *

Edward's birth caught me in the midst of a soul-searching crisis. During the first few rotations of my internship, working twelve hours on a good day and twenty-four hours on a bad one, I sighed with pleasure at the thought of my chosen career in ophthalmology. The loss of sleep was wearing me down, and yet, in the midst of those frantic days and nights, a longing began to gnaw at me. The life-and-death struggles that drove me to the brink of collapse also gave me something precious, something I didn't want to surrender. In the eyes of the mother of a dying child, there lurks a special depth, a special meaning. When those eyes gaze at the doctors who care for her child, they glow with gratitude and respect. In the surgical ICU, a patient who has just vomited a pint of blood doesn't ignore the doctor at his bedside. No, he reaches out a desperate hand. The patient cannot speak, he gags on the Sengstaken-Blakemore Occluder thrust down his throat to staunch a massive esophageal hemorrhage, but his eyes say it all: *Please help me, Doctor. Please don't let me die.*

Night after night, stumbling from ward to ward, I craved those pleading eyes, those hands that grasped my own with a passion known only to the mortally ill. I wanted to give my patients the most precious gift of all—life. The noblest physician, the surgeon with a knife and the skill to use it, wields a force like no other. His patients never ignore him. But the knife and the skill are not enough. A surgeon must sentence himself to a grueling lifelong struggle, fearing the moment when a slip of his knife or his mind will kill a patient. As I watched my colleagues split an abdomen with a sweep of the scalpel, slicing through skin and fat and muscle to expose a cancerous tumor, I coveted their skills. My affection for the immaculate world of ophthalmology—a world inhabited by phony surgeons, or so it seemed—had begun to wane. I coveted the true surgeon's power over life and death, but could I pay the price?

Edward Brown became a special patient. At his bedside, I would discover the secret that decided my fate. Rushing upstairs to the OB ward, I kept prodding my memory to explain the nurse's absurd phrase—"guts falling out"—but to no avail. After four years of medical school, I still had no clue what disaster awaited me.

The mother lay on the OB ward, her eyes closed, her disheveled hair damp from the sweat of her labor. The father sat by her bedside, his face buried in his hands, his shoulders heaving with the rhythmic thrust of his sobs. Edward lay in the delivery room, a small baby with spindly limbs and sunken cheeks. His head was bald except for scattered ringlets of dark hair. His translucent skin showed only the faintest trace of color—an almond tint, perhaps? Or was it the almond shape of his wide-open eyes that hangs in my memory, or the peculiar whiff that caught my nostrils—almonds, again? The child sucked on a pacifier and gazed at the mysterious ceiling above his bassinet. Someone had covered his abdomen with what appeared to be a mound of wet surgical drapes.

The OB nurse scowled at me.

"Dammit all!" she said. "I told that page operator it was really bad, and she should send the resident. Look at this." She lifted the drapes to expose a glistening, churning mass of intestines, a mass so bulky it dwarfed the infant lying beneath it. I stood astonished, gazing down at the child. "Now you believe me?" She said. "You better get that resident of yours up here STAT!"

"OK, OK," I said, rushing for the door. "I'll get him right away."

* * *

When I first met Ames Miller, I thought him an idiot. He was short, had a flat head, a square jaw, and almost no neck. At our first morning rounds, a nurse remarked in a whispered aside, "Why does the poor man wear his hair in a flattop?" She was right. The combined effect of his skull, jaw, and hair brought the word "blockhead" to the tip of the tongue. But Ames proved himself an intelligent man, though he loved children with what I judged an irrational passion. Infants were his favorite. Not content with the dozens of sick kids heaped upon him every workday, he had a three-year-old son at home, born during his third year of medical school. Six months before we met, his wife had delivered what he described—his face shining with delight—as "another little shitter." Before rounds, when he traded tales with two nurses who also had infants at home, the topic often drifted to excretory events. One morning Ames boasted that his sweet new daughter had managed to anoint her curly locks with a whole fistful of stool.

Ames was a second-year resident, far more learned than I in pediatric matters, but he shared my ignorance of a newborn with his guts falling out. Shown Edward's deformity, he gaped and fled just as I had. The surgical resident on call that night, a well-groomed Syrian named Ahmed, brought the first note of authority to those dismal proceedings. He was slim and poised and spoke with a cultured accent. The OB nurse, angry that we hadn't summoned a more senior surgeon, stood glowering beside Edward's bassinet, her jaw set and her arms crossed on her chest.

Ahmed smiled at her, said, "Let's see what we have here," then lifted the drapes from Edward's abdomen. In the first instant, his jaw dropped and his eyebrows shot up, but his face soon regained its masklike composure. "Oh, my," he said, gently lowering the drapes. "Congenital gastroschisis—a very bad case." He paused and blinked a few times.

Ames and I stared at him, waiting for a glimmer of hope, a miracle that might bail us out of this catastrophe.

"Be sure to dose him up with ampicillin." Ahmed said. "And keep those drapes wet with sterile saline. We don't want his intestines to get dried out or infected."

At last poor Edward had a diagnosis: gastroschisis, a congenital defect in the abdominal wall through which his naked intestines had prolapsed into the outside world. Adding to his troubles, the nooselike constriction of the defect had caused massive congestion, creating a mound twice the size of Edward's head, while the raw, glistening surface of the swollen bowels offered an appetizing target for bacteria.

Ahmed's pronouncement disturbed Edward, or so it seemed, for the moment the room fell silent, he began to fret. He balled his tiny fists, screwed his eyes shut, and spat out the pacifier, then gave a feeble cry that sounded like the quack of a baby duck. His thin legs stirred beneath the drape-covered mound.

"Oh, Doctor," the nurse said, grasping Ahmed's arm as he threw his latex gloves into a trash can and headed for the door. "What formula should we feed him? Do you recommend Similac or Enfamil?"

"My God, no, you..." Ahmed said, catching himself a hairsbreadth short of adding "you fool." Even Ames and I had sorted that one out: the last thing Edward's strangulated intestines needed was a digestive challenge. A bottle of formula would surely finish him off.

"But...but, Doctor," the nurse said, "what are we going to do?"

"Well, I...uh, yes..." Ahmed stammered, holding the door open with one hand. He turned toward the nurse, then paused. His gaze shifted to Edward, who was waving his limbs and giving tiny, quacklike cries. "Draw some blood, run a 'crit, get a CBC, start an IV with half normal saline."

"Yes, Doctor," she said, "but then...then what?"

Ahmed shook his head. His smooth face and slim body seemed to sag.

"I...I don't know."

No one spoke. The nurse, Ames, Ahmed, and I stood scattered around the delivery room, amid tables and cabinets and the implements of childbirth. We all looked at Edward. We heard his feeble cries. We saw his tiny arms and legs flailing about. I couldn't know the thoughts of the others, but mine were dark indeed: *Guard your heart, you foolish man, for that child will soon be dead.*

* * *

It was a failure of imagination. Indeed, how could anyone imagine a cure for that deformed child, whose shrunken abdominal cavity, no larger than a tennis ball, could never contain those swollen yet vital organs? Ahmed was poised and bright, learned in the ways of the surgeon. His crestfallen retreat had removed all hope. Edward's fate seemed no better than that of a death-row inmate, except the moment of his demise—from infection, infarction, or heaven knew what catastrophe—remained unknown. I tried to flee, but Ames beat me to it.

"Wait," I said as he headed for the door. "Aren't you going to start an IV?"

"What's your problem, Gamel? Aren't you the big IV hotshot in this hospital?"

The door of the delivery room flapped on its hinges, and he was gone. As his comment suggested, I fancied myself the most skilled phlebotomist among my internship class. Several colleagues, upon hearing tales of my dexterity, had asked me to start an IV or perform a lumbar puncture after their own efforts failed. My special triumph came with scalp-vein IVs, tiny needles threaded into the scalps of infants whose wasted limbs offered no trace of a decent blood vessel. A month before Edward's arrival, I had earned the nickname "Dracula" by drawing blood from a microscopic vein on the scalp of a three-pound preemie, yet I needed—for desperate personal reasons—to stay away from Edward.

I steeled myself. *Let's play a game*, I thought—*let's pretend this isn't a human being.* In my mind's eye, I struggled to transform Edward into an alien life form, a creature so strange and unlovely it could lay no claim on my affections. One-by-one, I wrapped a tourniquet around each of his pathetic limbs. My palpating finger discovered no trace of a vein, but the instant I touched him, he fell silent, as though my squeezing and stroking his flesh brought a primal comfort. His limbs lay still and his eyes opened wide, like the eyes of a child filled with wonder. When I replaced the pacifier between his lips, an eager suck snatched it from my fingers. He gave a flurry of grunts and sucks, then settled into a contented silence.

The time had come. I had no choice: the ritual of the scalp-vein IV must begin. The OB nurse laid an IV tray on the table beside Edward's bassinet. I took a rubber band from the tray, gently lifted Edward's head, stretched the band until it circled just above his ears, then snapped it in place. A network of swollen veins raced across his scalp. I peered closely, assisted by a bright overhead light, searching for the plumpest specimen, until—ah, yes, there lay a juicy vein the size of a pencil lead running two inches above the rubber band. I grabbed a can of shaving cream, worked a dollop into the hair overlying the chosen vein, shaved the hair from a patch of scalp using a safety razor, and painted the skin with Betadine. Finally, I reached for the butterfly, a needle attached to two winglike plastic tabs that help anchor it in place.

I steadied my nerves with a slow, deep breath. The chosen vein was no larger than the 21-gauge needle pinched between my thumb and index finger. If I failed, the surgeons would have to perform a cut-down—slice open Edward's arm or leg in search of a vein large enough to hold the life-sustaining needle. The bloody procedure, stressful even for a healthy newborn, would carry a special risk for Edward. I exchanged an anxious glance with the

OB nurse. She braced Edward's head between her hands. As the needle pierced his translucent skin and threaded its way across his scalp, I took care to enter the diaphanous vein at a shallow angle, lest the sharp tip tear it to shreds. The needle found its mark. Edward's dark blood flowed into the two specimen vials, and soon an IV bottle was dripping the half-normal saline that would sustain his life during the coming weeks.

But in the midst of triumph, disaster crept upon me. As I pierced Edward's flesh, holding my breath to steady my hand, the shield-wall around my heart gave way. Perhaps it was the euphoria brought on by a devilish challenge well-met. Perhaps it was the terrible closeness, my face hovering inches from his doll-like features, from the wide, pale eyes that grew wider still the instant my needle punctured his scalp. His eyes teared, his breathing sputtered, and the sucking stopped, but he did not squall or strain against the nurse's hands. By the time I had taped the butterfly in place, then taped a clear plastic medicine cup over it to protect against an accidental bump, I was a goner. The brave creature had caught me. In the flash of a moment, it felt as though he were my own child.

* * *

Early the next morning, the surgery service swooped down and stole Edward from me. Fair enough—there was nothing more I could do for him. The hospital's library contained only a few articles on gastroschisis, and these did little more than speculate on the embryological derangement that brought it about. *Archives of Disease in*

Childhood opined, "This defect is the result of obstruction of the omphalomesenteric vessels during development." Which is to say, the embryonic tissue meant to form the abdominal wall had lost its blood supply, then melted away from lack of oxygen. My spirits sank when I saw pictures of infants with only one or two loops of bowel prolapsing through a tiny umbilical defect. Neat, no problem: slit open the umbilicus, tuck the loops back in, sew up the wound. But, as Ahmed had noted, Edward suffered a bad case: every inch of his swollen digestive tract lay in a pile beneath those drapes. What on earth could anyone do to save him?

He was transferred to the east nursery, where I looked in on him many times a day, until the word got out that Professor DeVries, Stanford's world-renowned pediatric surgeon, would soon come to operate on Edward. I questioned Ahmed, then spoke with an intern on the Stanford surgery service, but neither had any idea what the great professor planned to do. I decided he would probably try to cover those bowels with a skin graft—a disturbing thought, since a huge patch of skin would be needed, and the resulting bulbous sack would leave Edward with a hideous lifelong deformity.

I felt terrible. The mental image of that sack revolted me, while the news that DeVries was taking over the case gave me bad vibes. The man was a pompous twit. I had never met him face-to-face, but he had lectured to my class during our third year of medical school, and on the podium he pranced around like a prima donna, so full of himself he seemed ready to burst. And he was tall, broad-shouldered, revoltingly handsome. Every time he stepped up to the lecture podium, the women in my class sighed and twittered. According to his CV, he had grown up in Iowa, but during a fellowship in pediatric surgery at Oxford University, the snob had acquired a British accent. In his lectures, he kept mentioning his "shedule," which I later discovered was the British pronunciation of "schedule." I hated to see Edward cared for by such a vain, self-absorbed man.

The operation took all morning. When I finally rushed up after peds clinic, I found a dozen doctors and nurses lined up at the window of the east nursery. The other bassinets were filled with preemies on respirators, so tiny and wasted they looked like hairless rats. Compared to these, Edward seemed robust, but my God, what was that? Something loomed over him as he lay in the bassinet, something huge and white and bizarre, made of what looked like laminated plastic. It took me several moments to sort out the astounding truth: DeVries had sewn the tip of an enormous funnel into Edward's abdomen.

Later that night, I returned to the nursery and lifted the wet gauze covering the top of the funnel. There lay Edward's swollen intestines, but the glistening mass... was it—yes! During the few hours since surgery, the mass had already begun to shrink. The swollen loops of bowel were smaller, approaching the size of normal intestines. DeVries had relieved the constriction by stretching the abdominal opening around the broad tip of the funnel, and now the force of gravity was draining the engorged lymph back into Edward's body.

This was not the end of Edward's perilous journey. There was still the problem—what seemed to me the insoluble problem—of that tiny abdominal cavity, which could hold only a fraction of the child's viscera, even when they had shrunk to normal size. I kept my vigil, stopping several times a day to gaze through the window of the preemie ward. Here I saw Edward's parents. They sat—gowned, gloved, and masked—in chairs beside his bassinet, taking turns stroking his cheek or holding his tiny hands. The two of them looked alike—thin in face and body, with elfin features that left no doubt Edward had come from their loins.

When they gazed at Edward—which the mother did often, the father seldom—their faces showed a quizzical uncertainty. The gadget erupting from their son's abdomen must have disturbed them, while every day bacteria hungered for those exposed organs, threatening to melt them into a soupy, infected hash. And surely the parents must have wondered, as I did, when—if ever—those organs would nestle into his tiny abdomen.

DeVries knew something we didn't: the tissues of a newborn retain an astounding plasticity. Day by day, then week by week, Edward's viscera settled deeper into the funnel as his abdomen slowly expanded. On two occasions he spiked a fever, the sign of an occult infection, but each time a change in the antibiotic regimen conquered the invading bacteria. All the while I rooted for the brave child who lay sucking on his pacifier hour after hour, his gaze fixed on the immense white funnel towering above him.

Since Edward had to remain NPO until those intestines were safely sewn inside his abdomen, his only nutrition came through my butterfly IV. The tiny needle, inserted by my hand into a tiny vein, was all that kept him alive. But no IV lasts forever. A nurse on the preemie ward told of a visit DeVries made two weeks after I had inserted the IV. Two weeks is the official limit; beyond that milestone, the risk of an infection around the needle begins to soar.

DeVries and Ahmed stood beside Edward's bassinet, staring down at my scalp-vein IV while the surgical intern laid out the instruments they would use to cut open an arm or leg in search of a new vein. No doubt DeVries noticed the child's limbs were now more spindly than ever, thanks to the wasting suffered by anyone who cannot take oral nourishment. The great surgeon hesitated. Moment by moment, as he examined those bony limbs, his eagerness to slice into one of them faded. Then, according to the nurse who told the story, he gingerly untaped the medicine cup shielding my IV and tipped it to one side. The surrounding skin showed the stubble of Edward's regrowing hair, but there was no redness or discharge to suggest infection.

"Hmm…well…" DeVries said, taping the cup back in place. "This looks pretty good. Keep an eye on it. Let me know if you see any pus, but we don't need to push our luck." Ahmed gave a sign of relief and repacked the instruments.

The story cheered me up. My achievement, a scalp-vein IV of exceptional longevity, had demanded only modest skill, but it bound me to Edward. I was part of his team, a secret sharer in his victory over what I and many others had thought was certain death. Thanks to DeVries' sleight of hand, an act of conjury more astounding than anything seen on a magician's stage, the child was climbing out of his coffin. Now, even a coward like me could unleash his affection. Week after shining week, Edward reigned as the hero of Valley Medical Center. Members of the hospital staff came by to watch the miracle unfold. His parents, sitting beside Edward's bassinet, smiled at the crowd gathered along the window.

In truth, my visits to the nursery, interludes snatched from hectic days and nights on the pediatric rotation, had as much to do with me as they did with Edward. The precious child's fate haunted me, but so did the sheer mechanics of that funnel. How in the hell did DeVries pull it off? In my mind's eye, I saw his forceps grasp the delicate membranes of Edward's abdominal wall and stretch them around that stiff plastic cone, taking care not to tear the tissue or trap a friable loop of bowel. A single misplaced stitch could have caused a raging peritonitis. How had that egomaniac acquired such skillful hands? And how did he live—how did he eat and sleep and endure the daily routines of life—knowing that the surgery he had done yesterday or would do tomorrow might fail, spelling the doom of an innocent child? A surgeon—a true surgeon—must endure a lifetime of stress, a career tormented by endless uncertainty.

No—the life of the knife was not for me. Better to steal away into the orderly universe encompassed by the human eye. Blindness was bad enough, but with any luck, I would not have to answer for death.

* * *

I missed Edward's final victory. It took two months for his viscera to settle into his abdomen, allowing DeVries to close the wound at last, and by then my internship had ended. I was in my first year of ophthalmology residency when word came up to Stanford that Edward had been discharged from the Valley Medical Center. For the next five years I gave him little thought, but then he crept back into my life. Not the literal Edward, but his spirit.

It happened at the Armed Forces Institute of Pathology in Washington, D.C., where I spent a two-year fellowship studying ophthalmic pathology, a rarefied specialty devoted to the histologic study of the eye and its surrounding tissues. I was in the library working on a manuscript when I noticed a copy of *The American Journal of Surgery* on an adjacent table. The lead article had an intriguing title: "Gastroschisis: the Long-Term Clinical Course of 29 Patients." To my delight, the authors reported that following surgical repair, the majority of patients enjoyed normal lives, indeed lives that could not be distinguished from those of their healthy peers.

I turned the page, and a picture in the article caught my eye. It showed a five-year-old child, about the age Edward would have been. The eyes in the photograph were blacked out to conceal the patient's identity, but the elfin features and hollow cheeks so resembled Edward's, they gave me a shock. The patient wore only jockey shorts. He had thin limbs and a bony, narrow chest. The shorts were pulled down to reveal an abdominal scar only three or four inches across. So there he stood, a living miracle—a child who could turn somersaults and leap about a playground like every other kid, with nothing more than a palm-sized scar to mark his horrendous entrance into this world.

CHAPTER FOURTEEN

The Elegant Eyeball

They aren't what most people think they are. Human eyes, touted as ethereal objects by poets and novelists throughout history, are nothing more than white spheres, somewhat larger than your average marble, covered by a leatherlike tissue known as sclera and filled with nature's facsimile of Jell-O. Your beloved's eyes may pierce your heart, but in all likelihood they closely resemble the eyes of every other person on the planet. At least I hope they do, for otherwise he or she suffers from severe myopia (nearsightedness), hyperopia (farsightedness), or worse.

Such uniformity is essential; for an eye to focus properly, its length and optical system must match to within a fraction of a millimeter. When a man and woman toss their genes together to make a baby, nature sets the focal point (determined by the optical power of the cornea and crystalline lens) at a standard distance, then adjusts the length of the eyeball to that same distance—twenty-four millimeters, or about one inch, with a few millimeters of variation thrown in for good measure. Thus, unlike livers and kidneys and hearts and brains—those ordinary, nonspherical organs—eyes tend to an impressive sameness all over the world. My spleen may be half again bigger than yours, while intestines can vary by five feet in length, but healthy eyes are like so many peas in a pod.

Trust me. I've handled hundreds of eyeballs, removed from their owners for a variety of unpleasant reasons. One of my jobs—that of the ophthalmic pathologist—is to slice these globes into wafer-thin strips, stain the strips with vivid colors (hematoxylin and eosin, periodic acid schiff, Masson trichrome), then examine the results under a microscope. Given these credentials, I can assure you that your lover's eyes differ from those of your most despised enemy only in the color and texture of the iris and in the size of the pupil. When we wax eloquent about "beautiful eyes," we are usually moved more by the trimmings—the lids, the lashes, the brows, the prominence of the globes in their orbits—than by anything contained within the eyes themselves. The Japanese sometimes refer to Westerners as "big eyes," an illusion caused by the lid position and orbital structure of Occidentals, while in truth the Japanese exhibit a collective tendency toward myopia that gives them on average slightly larger eyeballs.

* * *

During my final year of medical school, I encountered the ultimate decision: to what specialty would I devote my life? Should I tend to phlegmy children who wriggle and scream when I thrust an otoscope into their ear? Should I slice open bellies, wander among livers and spleens and gallbladders, grope my way through greasy omental fat to explore coil after coil of diseased intestines? Or should I tend to the human heart, throbbing in its nest between the foamy pink lungs?

I flirted with cardiology, then settled on neurology. Nothing rivals the complexity of the human brain, I reasoned, and there is no more noble goal than curing its various ailments. Here was the ultimate dialectic: using the skilled synapses of my own brain, I would diagnose and cure the diseased brains of others. Fortunately, while taking a six-week elective on the neurology service, I made a horrifying discovery: their ward was filled with zombies. Almost every patient suffered from a stroke, a seizure, or a brain tumor, and they rarely got better. If we finally diagnosed a curable lesion, we had to ship the patient off to the neurosurgeons. By the end of the elective, I felt like a zombie myself.

Ophthalmology? A clean, precise specialty that offered its own dialectic. With my intact eye, I would diagnose and cure the diseased eyes of others. It didn't take long, only one glimpse into the ocular depths through a dilated pupil, and my quest was finished. There before me lay a stunning panorama—a lacework of arteries and veins spread on a burnt-umber palate swirled and streaked with delicate shades of ocher. Most spectacular of all was the retina, a transparent wafer that gleamed like polished glass under the light of my ophthalmoscope. In the center, the optic nerve shone like a risen sun.

I was smitten.

When my internship ended, I was eager to immerse myself in the nuances of the eye. The senior residents showed me fabulous glimpses of the cornea, lens, and retina—a panorama of shades and textures that rivaled the most gorgeous sunset—yet months elapsed before I acquired the dexterity to bring those images into sharp focus. When I sliced into a living eyeball, the operating microscope transformed the slightest tremor into an earthquake, while one slip of the razor-sharp knife might blind the patient forever.

Of all the nerve-wracking challenges, retrobulbar injection topped the list. During this procedure, I had to thrust a needle through the lower eyelid, around the equator of the globe, then deep into the cone of muscles behind the eye. After watching others do it for several months, I began injecting patients to numb them for laser treatment or cataract surgery. They were terrified.

"My God, Doc, it feels like you're jamming that needle right in my eye!"

Nor was their fear without reason: an unskilled hand could pierce the globe or rip a hole in the optic nerve. Our chairman planted a poisoned seed in my mind when he warned, "On average, you're going to stick the eye about once in every 3,000 shots." The statistic haunted me for the rest of my career. Despite 10,000 successful injections, every time I picked up the needle, a voice inside my head warned, "Be careful. This could be the day your luck runs out."

The chance to do harm waited at every turn. I hardly slept the night before my first cataract operation, going over and over again the techniques I had learned by practicing on cow eyes. Our sutures were finer than a human hair, almost invisible to the unaided eye, but through the operating microscope, they looked like ropes. A knot properly tied brought a rush of satisfaction, while a misplaced stitch contorted the tiny wound.

"Cut it loose," the attending surgeon muttered under his mask, keeping his voice low to avoid arousing the sedated patient. "Try again, and get it right this time."

I knew if I failed again, or if my hands trembled too wildly, he would take over the case. Patient care remained the first priority, but surrendering a case to the attending meant even more anxiety the next time I picked up a knife.

Fear proved a vital part of my training. After decades spent learning, practicing, and teaching, I realized this is as it should be. When derived from a rational source, anxiety serves a vital purpose. Anyone who operates on a patient's eye must keep her mind focused every moment. She must prepare, she must think, and she must care about the patient. By this train of logic, I would argue that a fearless surgeon is a dangerous creature.

* * *

Since every normal eye displays a clear cornea and a white scleral coat, any notion of special beauty attributed to the globe itself must derive from the iris, the dynamic membrane that contains the pupil and rests in front of the crystalline lens. The iris comes in many colors, but according to the potboilers and bodice-rippers of English fiction, the most beautiful irises are always blue: light blue, velvety blue, ice-blue, welkin-eyed, peacock, midnight, cobalt. Green gets an occasional nod—"She had jewel-bright emerald eyes, so lustrous and fetching they tore through my heart"—but most of the time blue runs the show. The rankest discrimination, and a bit ironic, since blue irises contain no intrinsic pigment, showing only the raw color of the tissue itself. The pigment cells in the Caucasian iris often add a twist to this aesthetic by lying dormant during the first few years of life, causing many parents to suffer a broken heart when the gorgeous blue eyes of their newborn turn muddy brown.

The texture of the iris is all but invisible to the unaided eye, but the ophthalmologist's slit-lamp microscope discloses a panorama of diaphanous spokes, crypts, and valleys—flecks, spots, and strands that dance about with each twitch of the pupil. Dark irises tend toward a tight weave, while light irises fluff up like a shag rug. And there's the all-important pupil—constricted by morphine and bright light, dilated by fear, darkness, sexual arousal, and death. Yes, the coroner's final measure, the mark of a departed soul—enormous black pupils that give nary a twitch even in the brightest light. Despite this morbid sign, many cultures consider large pupils a sign of beauty. The Spanish give the name belladonna ("beautiful lady") to a poisonous, pupil-dilating drug extracted from the plant *Atropa belladonna*, more commonly known as deadly nightshade.

A note on cosmetics: under an ophthalmologist's microscope, false lashes look like mutilated telephone poles, while mascara shows up as greasy black lumps that squiggle across the corneal tear film with every blink. For the efficiency-minded woman, there is permanent eyeliner, a dark line tattooed along the lid margin. It works beautifully, provided styles don't change, and provided the tattooist, working millimeters from the cornea, doesn't inject ink into the eyeball.

About myopia—if you have it, be happy. Numerous scientific studies have shown that nearsighted men and women boast a higher average intelligence than their nonmyopic cohorts. This association could reflect either nature or nurture. Naturists argue that during embryogenesis, the eyes develop from the same neural tube as the brain. Since large eyes tend to be myopic, big eyes and big brains might go together in much the same fashion as long arms and long legs. Nurturists, on the other hand, insist that myopia leads to high intelligence because of its effect on early childhood development. Most nearsighted kids wander around undiagnosed for years, and during this formative period—unable to see the baseballs, Frisbees, and rocks thrown at them by their playmates—they spend a lot of time indoors. The nonathletic myopes who take up reading get high scores on their SATs, while those who take up eating give us claustrophobia by overflowing the seat next to us on airplanes. Myopia also exerts a powerful influence on career choice, as evidenced by the 85 percent of my fellow ophthalmologists who are myopic, an incidence far greater than that of the normal population. Pathology breeds preoccupation.

* * *

However beautiful the human eye, it serves a more important purpose than romantic allure. Forty percent of the brain is devoted to vision, which provides us with more information than our other four senses combined. Our optic nerves transmit millions of impulses to the brain every second that specify the location, color, and intensity of light for all the points in our visual space. Even more impressive is our visual cortex, which fuses the slightly disparate images from each eye to give us the three-dimensional miracle known as depth perception. A stunning feat, since video cameras, arguably the benchmark of modern technology, can muster only two dimensions.

Certain ocular tissues stand on the pinnacle of evolution. How does nature, so crude in claw and fang, create a surface that brings light to a pinpoint focus? This surface must be perfectly curved, perfectly transparent, perfectly smooth. It must be—water! Which is to say, the cornea owes its optical precision to a tear film whose dissolved salts, lipids, and proteins allow it to maintain a flawless wetted surface. A man who has no tears stands on the threshold of blindness. And that man will writhe in agony, since a bone-dry cornea responds to each blink with a jolt of pain so terrible, sufferers compare it to rubbing shards of glass on the eye.

Another evolutionary triumph: for light to reach the retina unimpeded, the cornea and lens must remain transparent, and yet, like all living tissues, they must be nourished by oxygen. More than 99.9 percent of all human cells obtain their oxygen from capillary blood flow, but capillaries lacing through the cornea and lens would veil our vision with opaque strands. To remain transparent, the outer portion of the cornea must survive on oxygen absorbed from the surrounding air, while the lens and the inner cornea depend on a colorless fluid known as aqueous, which flows through the chambers of the eye. Normal aqueous contains neither hemoglobin nor cells of any sort, thus it carries only a tiny fraction of the oxygen contained in blood. And the rate of aqueous flow must be precisely controlled: a deficiency shrivels the eye into a useless spitball, while blockage of the trabecular drainage channels near the base of the iris leads to throbbing pain and blindness. Thus normal vision, the presumed birthright of every human being, demands an array of tissues more complex and wondrous than anything crafted by man.

* * *

Of all the ugly things in this world, I would argue that diseases top the list: cancer, syphilis, leprosy, gangrene, fungating ulcers. Even the pictures lying flat and odorless on the pages of a textbook bring a surge of revulsion. And let us not forget elephantiasis, an infestation by wriggling filarial worms that block the lymphatic channels, causing the legs to swell up like tree trunks. Some male victims pay an especially painful price, forced to carry their massive scrotum before them in a wheelbarrow.

But surely the eye, the most delicate of organs, is afflicted by only the subtlest diseases. Or so one might think. I soon discovered the fallacy of this logic. In truth, some of the most grotesque diseases are those that disfigure the eye. Ophthalmology did not prove the sanitary refuge I had hoped for.

* * *

During the first week of my residency, I examined Justine Kimbro, a tall, slender diabetic in her late teens. She was accompanied by a tall mother who carried twice her daughter's bulk. Justine complained, "My eyes are full of floaters." *Good,* I thought. *Floaters. No problem.* Everything looked fine from the outside—white sclera, clear corneas, pale blue irises. Then I focused my ophthalmoscope through her dilated pupils. "Excuse me," I said, and stepped out of the room.

By that time in my career, I had seen the interior of a few-dozen eyes, each a breathtaking panorama of amber and brown, yellow and pink, shading through a delicate lacework of arteries and veins. But Justine's eyes were filled with tangles of angry red spiders. Dark clots rose into the vitreous gel, trailing streamers of blood in all directions. I stepped into the hall to grab Doug Jacobson, the retina specialist in clinic that morning. It took only an instant. Doug focused the beam of his ophthalmoscope on Justine's right eye, then her left. He removed the ophthalmoscope from his head and hung it on the wall.

"You have diabetic retinopathy," he said. "And I'm sorry to say it's very advanced."

The mother burst into tears.

"Oh, Doctor," she sobbed, "my grandmother, my cousin Ernest, this woman across the street—so many people I know went blind from diabetes! Can't you do something?"

Justine said nothing. Her wide-open eyes were dry, the irises stretched into pale blue rims around the blackness of her dilated pupils. Later, in private, Jacobson gave me her diagnosis in the vernacular—

jungle-osis. Jungle-osis meant dense black clots, arching streamers of blood, a traction retinal detachment bound with scars so dense they defy even the most skillful surgeon. Jungle-osis also meant blindness in both eyes, and soon—weeks, perhaps a month or two. Justine, not yet twenty years of age, was doomed to stumble through the remaining decades of her life with a white cane or a guide dog. Nor was blindness the end of her troubles. She might develop absolute glaucoma, an inexorable rise in pressure so nauseating and painful, victims often beg to have their eyes removed.

But, perhaps not. Justine's only hope was a treatment so new we had no proof it worked, a treatment whose promise was based on the crudest evidence. For decades, ophthalmologists had noted a strange phenomenon: when one eye of a diabetic showed widespread retinal scars from an old injury or infection, that eye always retained vision long after hemorrhages had blinded the other eye. Apparently, by a mechanism no one understood at the time, these scars protected the surviving retinal tissue from the ravages of diabetes.

Thus by logic that might impress a blacksmith or a witchdoctor, the new treatment called for obliterating much of the nonessential peripheral retina in an effort to save the central portion that gives us our sharpest vision. Since there was no other option, Jacobson advised Justine—a girl speechless with fear, perched on the brink of blindness—to let us experiment on her.

Just months before Justine's arrival, our clinic had acquired the Coherent Radiation Model 800, the first commercial laser designed for treating the human eye. Its console, shaped like a coffin, stood three feet high and six feet long. A glass tube buried deep within its circuitry emitted a high-pitched whine and an eerie bluish-green beam of light. Shown against a wall, the beam formed a circle of shimmering motes that scurried about like atoms in a nuclear furnace. A fabulous instrument, more precise than any razor, but now its tightly focused beam would serve a crude purpose—destroying retinal tissue. By the dozens, by the hundreds, the laser emitted tiny flashes, each flash the space-age equivalent of a magnifying lens burning a hole in a leaf. When the treatment was complete, lifeless white scars obliterated half of the patient's peripheral retina. Care was taken to avoid the vital central portion, assuring that if the treatment worked, the patient would maintain the acute vision needed to read and drive a car.

Justine suffered. To dull the pain from those hundreds of burns, we injected Xylocaine deep behind her eye. The contact lens used to deliver the laser beam sometimes caused a painful corneal abrasion. For three or four days after every treatment, fluid leaking from the peripheral burns seeped into the central retina, blurring and distorting her vision. Justine's mother was always there, wringing her hands and squeezing her eyes shut when her daughter moaned under our long needle. But after six treatments, the vitreous hemorrhages began to clear. The tangle of spiders melted away.

Nine months after Justine's first visit, Jacobson announced, "That's it. All the hemorrhage is gone."

Justine's mother burst into tears, dropped her purse on the floor, and threw her arms around Jacobson. His face blushed fiery red as he struggled against her grip, muttering, "No, no, it's too soon to tell for sure," but he was a small man, half a head shorter and many pounds lighter than the joyful mother.

During the last months of my residency, Justine's vision remained 20/20 in both eyes. There was no trace of hemorrhage, nor of the spidery vessels that signal recurrent proliferative retinopathy.

Over the next three decades, cures like Justine's would number in the hundreds of thousands as laser therapy became the gold standard for treating diabetic retinopathy. Adding to this miracle was the discovery that, following an adequate treatment, patients almost never relapsed. A study published in 1976 showed a fourfold reduction in severe visual loss, but further modifications to the original method have all but eliminated total blindness among diabetics. By the end of the twentieth century, numerous charities had delivered improved versions of the Coherent Model 800 to developing nations across the globe, allowing millions of patients to enjoy its benefits.

In recent years, science finally discovered the once-mysterious mechanism by which the laser cures diabetic retinopathy. As with so many diseases of the eye and other organs, the culprit is oxygen deprivation. Diabetes obliterates the capillaries that sustain the retina's inner layers. The resulting lack of oxygen stimulates the release of vascular endothelial growth factor (VEGF), a compound that entices the retina to sprout a network of fragile new blood vessels. Rather than nourishing the retina, these vessels creep into the vitreous cavity, where they rupture and release massive clots. Dense bands of scar tissue then shrivel the retina into a useless lump. Laser treatment, by cauterizing nonessential portions of the retina, enhances blood flow to the central retina and reduces the secretion of VEGF. As a result, within days of the treatment, the abnormal blood vessels begin to melt away.

Laser surgery for proliferative retinopathy has proved a medical triumph of the first order. Here is something crude in principle, simple to perform, and easily learned, but it works. Though I had nothing to do with its discovery, over the course of my career I have treated thousands of patients, including numerous familial combinations: husband and wife, mother and son, father and son, and, in one instance, granddaughter and grandmother. Even more important than my own patients were the dozens of residents I taught to use the laser, who by now have treated thousands of their own patients. After three decades as a teacher, scientist, and physician, my role in the miracle that defeated jungle-osis remains the most satisfying privilege of my career.

CHAPTER FIFTEEN

Dangerous Doctors

I was not disturbed to find a giant man sitting alone in our waiting room, even though the Stanford Eye Clinic was not scheduled to open for half an hour and, the week before, an early morning intruder had accosted two nurses in the OB-GYN clinic down the hall. Nor was I disturbed that the man sat cross-legged on a prayer mat, eyes closed, wrists on knees, thumb and index finger pinched together—the asana posture—humming a long, steady mantra. This yogi was the tallest person I had ever seen. Even with his butt on the floor, his head came almost to my chest. He had a gaunt face and scraggly auburn beard. His sandy hair, tied in a ponytail, hung to the middle of his back. I felt myself in no physical danger, since the new-age radicals who swarmed over the San Francisco Peninsula during the 1970s were a peaceful lot, but one item disturbed me: he wore a white coat.

Bad news. It was the first Monday of the month, thus the white coat meant this might be our new medical student, come to spend a four-week elective in the Stanford Eye Clinic. As the chief resident, I had to deal with any problems that arose among our crew of two clerks, two technicians, three residents, and any students who happened to be hanging about.

Mine was already a troublesome job. At Stanford during that era, competent staff was hard to find, since official policy, in keeping with the liberality that flowed over Northern California like the cooling Pacific breeze, forbade the firing of anyone for any cause short of a felony conviction. As a result of such indulgence, ungifted employees wandered from clinic to clinic, descending the academic pyramid until they reached that department with the flabbiest political muscle. Thanks to our chairman, an overfed teddy bear, years of attrition had given the Stanford Eye Clinic a depressing assemblage of workers.

There was Bea Chalmers—Little Bea—our appointment clerk, a faded woman the color of soap, a grandmother at forty and already beginning to shrivel. She had a sweet rosebud smile and the perspicacity of a hammer. When a huckster in Texas announced that he had performed the world's first eye transplant—a gross exaggeration, in truth nothing more than an extra-large corneal graft—the *San Francisco Chronicle* ran a front-page headline: "Hope for the Hopelessly Blind." Our appointment phone rang for hours, with Little Bea assuring every caller, "Oh, yes, our doctors here at Stanford do those new eye transplants." Over the next few days, I found our waiting room filled with guide dogs and white canes. Dozens of hapless patients had been sucked in by Little Bea's abysmal naïveté. When told the terrible truth, some left in tears, others purple with rage at being so cruelly misled.

Then there was Althea, a technician who faked the visual fields she was meant to perform at each visit by copying the fields from previous visits, a ploy that saved her time but sabotaged the treatment of many glaucoma patients. The chairman fired Althea after discovering her dangerous ways, but Stanford's grievance committee harassed him with paperwork and obligatory meetings until he hired her back.

Sylvia, our other technician, had brassy red hair straight from the jar and a pathologically soft heart. When patients wept in frustration because they couldn't read a line on the visual acuity chart, she would coo, "Oh, poor thing. Tell me, honey, do those letters look like an *S* and an *L*?" If the patient replied, "Yes, yes, that's it!" she would dutifully record their vision as 20/200. One unfortunate patient—moments after Sylvia had recorded his acuity as 20/400, the big *E* on the eye chart—broke a tooth when he walked headlong into a doorjamb.

Bea, Althea, and Sylvia kept me frazzled enough. I didn't need a giant medical student who laid out his prayer rug in the waiting room and entertained our soon-to-arrive patients by humming his mantra—"ooohhhhmmm... ooohhhmmm...ooohhhmmm"— in a buzzing vibrato that rumbled like the bass pipe of a church organ. I waited. At last he fell silent and opened his eyes.

"Morgan Gillman," he said, leaping up to shake my hand. "How do you do? How do you do? How do you do?"

His enormous hand was cool and damp. I tilted my head back to gaze up at his lean bearded face. The man towered above me, every bit as tall as I had feared. An inadequate tie, bright with polka dots but soiled and badly knotted, hung halfway down his rumpled shirtfront. His Lincolnesque face was long and narrow, with hazel eyes that flitted about, fixing on my chin, my ear, my belt buckle, never on my eyes.

"You our new student?" I asked.

"Yes yes yes," he said, still pumping my hand, until at last I pulled it from his moist grip. He squatted to roll up his prayer mat. At that moment, Doug Jacobson grabbed my arm.

"Let's go," he said. "How many cases we got on this morning?"

Jacobson was no taller than a twelve-year-old. His high forehead and long, dark hair gave the startling impression of a Napoleonic dwarf. Before I could answer, he staggered back, gazing at Morgan as he rose to his astonishing height with the prayer mat tucked under his arm.

"How do you do? How do you do? How do you do?" Morgan said, leaning down to pump Jacobson's hand, nodding to and fro with each pump.

"I'm fine, thank you," Doug said, freeing his hand from Morgan's grip. He stared for a moment at Morgan's dirty necktie, which hung level with his eyes. "Oh, my," Doug mumbled under his breath, shaking his head in disbelief.

Morgan and I followed Doug into the laser room, which contained the Coherent Model 800. Morgan stopped in his tracks when he heard the eerie whine and saw the coffinlike console lurking in a shadowy corner.

"Ugh," he grunted, pointing at the console. "My God, what's that?"

"It's OK," I said. "Calm down. Just don't touch anything."

While a nurse led in the first patient and seated him at the laser slit-lamp, I explained to Morgan that during the treatment, the two of us would take turns viewing the patient's retina through a tubular eyepiece attached to the slit-lamp microscope. A volley of *click*s from the switch beneath Jacobson's right foot signaled the beginning of the treatment. With each *click*, a blue-green flash struck the retina, cauterizing it into a chalky white dot. Flash followed flash, *click-click-click-click*, as the white dots wove their way through a complex array of veins and arteries.

Morgan hunched down to look through the eyepiece, but the visual spectacle seemed to strain his nervous system. From his cavernous lungs came grunts, groans, and an occasional sigh. An anxious body odor filled the room—was it Morgan or the patient? A foreboding tingle crept up my spine, yet things kept *click*ing and moaning and sweating along until it was my turn at the eyepiece. When the moment arrived, Morgan stepped aside, lifted his foot to prop it on the yard-high laser console, then leaned his elbow on the delicate tube that focused the beam on the patient's retina. Through the eyepiece, I watched the laser beam skitter across the patient's retina.

Jacobson shouted, "Jesus Christ!"

I tugged at Morgan's bony shoulder and rose on tiptoe to whisper in his ear.

"Get down!" I warned. "Stay away from that console."

"I'm sorry, I'm sorry, I'm sorry," Morgan said. He took his foot from the console. A minute later he put it back and leaned on the tube.

Jacobson shouted, "Jesus Christ!"

I pulled at Morgan's shoulder and whispered another warning, but only moments later his mind wandered again. For the third time, his enormous foot thudded onto the laser console.

Jacobson shouted, "Jesus Christ! Get that man out of here!"

Jacobson's strident voice carried all over the clinic. I grabbed Morgan's arm and led him into a waiting room filled with startled patients. "That's one of my problems," he said, wringing his hands as he followed me into the clinic's coffee alcove. His long torso trembled. He clenched his jaw and backed into a corner, squirming against the walls. His face grew damp with sweat. "I just can't keep my mind focused. I took my medicine today, but only one pill. Doctor Cheever's very nice. We…we talked on the phone last night…I've been looking forward to ophthalmology 'cause I love eyeballs. Can…can I have lunch with you?"

"Doctor Cheever?" I said. "Isn't he in hematology?"

"Yes yes yes. He looks after me."

"Looks after you? You've got something wrong with your blood?"

"No, but he's a nice man. Very nice. He takes care of me."

Morgan's beard trembled inches above my forehead. I looked up into his sallow, anxious face. The poor man had no idea how normal people were meant to behave. He seemed desperate to flee—flee that clinic, that building, perhaps all of humanity. The two of us stood in silence. At last Doug Jacobson stepped into the alcove, blushed when he saw Morgan, then took my arm and tried to steer me aside, but Morgan thrust himself between us.

"Thank you, thank you, thank you," he said, pumping Jacobson's hand.

Jacobson jerked his hand away, rushed down the hall to his office, and slammed the door behind him. For the remainder of the morning, I let Morgan follow me around while I saw my patients. During the first three or four exams, he lurked in a corner, wringing his hands, silent except for an occasional hum or sigh. Then I examined a patient who had gone blind in his right eye the day before. My ophthalmoscope showed lumps of dark, clotted blood distorting the central retina. In the patient's other eye, a yellow scar had destroyed the central retina years before, and now all hope of useful vision was lost. I summoned Jacobson to confirm my findings. He examined the patient, an old farmer whose bald head was covered with liver spots, then stepped into the waiting area to gather the man's son, daughter, and grandson into the exam room. Morgan and I stood in the doorway.

"Sometimes," Jacobson said, laying his hand on the patient's arm, "macular degeneration gets away from us…

and when the eye hemorrhages, blood clots block the laser beam. There's nothing we can do. No treatment, no treatment at all."

The room fell silent. The patient's son, as bald and almost as wrinkled as his father, pressed his hand against his mouth. The patient's daughter sniffed and wiped her eyes. The grandson, a six-year-old in shorts and a blue beanie, sat perched on his mother's knee, staring at Jacobson with a solemn frown. The patient remained quiet, nodding his head as though to say, "Yes, I suspected as much."

Then came a noise—a deep, raucous explosion—right in my ear. It was Morgan. At first I thought he was choking on phlegm. "Uh hu hu hu hu…Uh hu hu hu…" He wrung his hands, writhed his body, rocking to and fro in wild gyrations. My God—Morgan was laughing! "Uh hu hu hu hu…" Everyone turned to stare. I stood paralyzed. At last I grabbed Morgan's arm and pulled him into the hall, leaving behind a room filled with black silence.

The rest of the morning passed in a daze. Lunch came at last. I found myself in an open courtyard of the hospital cafeteria, seated at a table with Bea, Sylvia, two junior residents, and Morgan. There in the glorious sunshine of a California spring—amid potted ferns, hanging planters, and the aroma of enchiladas and black bean soup—I racked my brain: what was I going to do with Morgan? For the moment, he seemed safe from mischief, seated beside me at the deserted end of the table. My companions, in an effort to stay far away from this strange creature, had crowded themselves down at the other end.

l forced a smile, laughed loudly, told jokes, struggling to engage my sane companions. At some point, Morgan turned away to chat with a passing acquaintance. Out of the corner of my eye, I saw his head bobbing, his scarecrow arms gesturing as he spoke. It was a relief to have him distracted, but midway through one of my excellent tales, my audience drifted away. They gaped, staring at something just to my right. Sylvia gave an ambiguous snort, something between a giggle and a scream. Little Bea, her eyes bulging, murmured, "My...my...my..."

I turned, and there sat Morgan—cheerful, verbose, more animated than I had ever seen him—talking to a potted fern. He laughed, slapped his knee, rocked back and forth.

"Uh hu hu hu hu...very good, Doctor Cheever...very good.... Uh hu hu hu hu...I agree...I agree..."

His eyes remained fixed on the fern, a man-sized plant drooping toward him from a concrete pot. That was it. I emptied my tray, ran upstairs to the eye clinic, and called the Office of Student Affairs. Busy. I called again. At last a woman answered.

"I need to talk to someone," I said. "It's about Morgan Gillman."

"Oh my God," she said. "Not him again."

* * *

Nancy Lyon was an administrative assistant in her late thirties, a stout albino with a round face and straight white hair. We had never met, but as she led me to her office, I felt a sense of intimacy—the shared trauma of two soldiers under attack by the same appalling enemy. The manila folder clutched under her arm proved a formality, lying unopened on the desk while she told Morgan's terrible story. He had been a brilliant college student, a physics major who graduated summa cum laude from an Ivy League school. His letters of recommendation described flawless grades and stunning achievements. His score on the Medical College Admissions Test was among the highest in the nation.

"When he decided to come to Stanford," Nancy said, "our admissions committee went ballistic. Everybody thought for sure Harvard would get him."

Stanford's labs and lectures posed no problem for Morgan. After breezing through the first two years of medical school, he broke the curve on Part I of the Medical Board Exam, but his first clinical rotation pushed him over the edge. On the pediatric ward, as his team gathered at the bedside of a child in the terminal stage of leukemia, Morgan announced that the FBI was transmitting threatening messages through a gold crown on one of his molars.

Three months on the psych ward and massive doses of Thorazine finally brought him back to earth. A week after his discharge—coherent and clear-eyed, at least for the moment—Morgan cut a deal. If he spent a year in psychotherapy, the dean of Stanford Medical School would allow him another chance to get his MD. But when the year of leave ended, Morgan was nowhere in sight. Even his parents had no idea what he was up to, but two years after his departure, Morgan knocked on the dean's door and declared himself healed, recovered, ready to begin again.

Where had he been all that time? In therapy, perhaps? Yes, Morgan said—at a peyote commune in Southern Mexico. The commune's "therapist," a Kadohadacho shaman, had insisted that Thorazine distorted Morgan's karma and put his chi into a tailspin. From now on, Morgan declared, he might or might not take his medicine, depending on the messages he received each day from the ether spirits.

Morgan's reenrolment in medical school brought a flurry of calls to the Office of Student Affairs. Neurology, then orthopedics, then pediatrics, all made frantic inquiries: who was this giant weirdo who showed up on their service in a white coat and declared himself a medical student? Morgan's demeanor, though always bizarre, remained fluid, evanescent—depending, I suspect, on the dose of Thorazine he had taken that day. On the orthopedics ward, he was Bartleby the Scrivener, aloof and withdrawn, standing motionless in a corner until someone led him away. In the pediatric clinic, amidst all those squalling infants, he arrived agitated, trembling and glassy-eyed, so obviously deranged the chief resident ordered security to take him straight down to the psych ward, where a four-week course of Thorazine brought him under control just in time to begin his ophthalmology rotation.

During the two years since his escapade at the peyote commune, Morgan had attempted six clerkships. Nancy was horrified because the dean had let this debacle drag on for so long, more horrified yet to learn Morgan had gotten credit for two of those clerkships. At this rate, in another year or two, he might have enough credits to graduate.

"He's insane," Nancy said. "How the hell can a lunatic get credit for a clinical rotation?"

How, indeed, especially at Stanford, one of the most prestigious medical schools in the country? A misadventure suffered by Dave Edwards, arguably the best student in my class (Stanford MD, 1971), might offer some insight into this debacle. A graduate of Cal Tec, David had been an aeronautical engineer before medical school and was the only student in our class who attended every single lecture. His fellow classmates loved him, since he allowed the slugabeds among us to photocopy his immaculate notes. Dave's straight-*A* career suffered a setback when the Stanford Cardiology Department awarded him a gentleman's *C* for his rotation. Though all his previous evaluations had been filled with lavish praise, this one noted only that he was an "adequate student." Dave's career could survive a minor blemish like that, but one fact disturbed him: he hadn't taken the cardiology elective.

In all likelihood, his evaluation form was sent to cardiology by mistake, and when no one in the department remembered him, an intern or resident copped out with a noncommittal grade. A lucky break for a student who signs up but never shows up or who shows up but gets chased off the first day because of his bizarre behavior. Then there was the jumble of red tape that fell about the neck of anyone brave enough to fail a student, as I discovered when I refused to give Morgan credit for his ophthalmology rotation.

Nancy assured me that if didn't fill out all the proper forms, or if I failed to show up for scheduled meetings with the dean's Student Committee, any breach in the protocol would be judged in the student's favor. Thus a persistent student, however inept or insane, might accumulate enough credits to graduate, provided every now and then, as he blunders through his clinical rotations, a harried resident or intern fails to do her duty. And there was Morgan, creeping ever closer toward a license to practice medicine.

But I did my duty, and my persistence paid off. Almost. After I described Morgan's fiascoes to the dean's Student Committee, they gave him a failing grade for the ophthalmology elective. During this process I met Doctor Cheever, Morgan's special advisor, a soft-spoken professor of hematology. No doubt his kind smile and warm grey eyes gave comfort at the bedside of his dying patients. I suspected someone in his family had suffered a disability, since he volunteered to be Morgan's advisor and served as his advocate at countless meetings. He spoke of Morgan's illness with passion in his voice.

"I've always felt the handicapped deserve special consideration. We can't blame Morgan for his failures. He's doing the best he can."

* * *

A year after finishing my residency, I returned to Stanford for a visit. Nancy had moved to San Diego, but Cheever was in his office. He greeted me with a forced smile that suggested anything but pleasure. We chatted for a while— where was I living, what was I up to?

"Well," he said at last, "I suppose you've come to hear about Morgan."

"Yes," I said, and remained silent, looking him in the eye. I didn't say, "Why did you dimwits keep tormenting the poor man with fantasies of becoming a doctor," but I thought it, and Cheever's defiant frown suggested he was reading my mind. The frown and the silence went on for a long time. Finally he dropped the bomb.

"Morgan got his MD last fall."

"What!" I blurted. "But...but...he's crazy as a loon. He won't take his medicine. My God, can you imagine..."

"Well, aren't you mister nice guy," he snarled, his face contorted with anger, as though I had shouted a string of racial epithets. "What would you have me do with the poor fellow? Say, 'Look, Morgan, you're crazy, and crazy people can't be doctors'? I'm not that kind of bastard. You can't blame the patient for his disease."

* * *

Cheever had a point: it wasn't Morgan's fault. No man would choose the torments that lurked behind those wild, jittery eyes. He had a special gift, but this gift carried with it a terrible burden. During the first year of medical school, he had aced a biochemistry midterm by regurgitating the Krebs Cycle down to the last minute detail, a feat no one in his class could match. According to a campus rumor, when asked how he accomplished this, Morgan replied, "I looked it up." Which is to say, he looked up the answer in the copy of *Basic Biochemical Pathways* recorded page by page in his photographic memory. His was a soaring intellect—indeed, a monstrous intellect. Perhaps a mind that records every pixel of the world around it is doomed to collapse from toxic overload. Or perhaps, by a cruel, immutable law, some geniuses must pay for their gift by hearing the blades of grass scream in agony when trodden underfoot.

Yet I must confess my sympathies do not lie entirely with Morgan Gillman. I cannot help but wonder: where is he now, and what has he done to his innocent patients?

CHAPTER SIXTEEN

The Bottom of the Pit

Mildred M., a receptionist and insurance clerk in the University of Louisville Eye Center, was a large, placid woman. She had a round face and a round body, with long dark hair that spread across her back like a tent. She was loyal, industrious, and trustworthy, but her face remained an unsmiling mask throughout the day, and her habit of chewing gum kept me in a state of distraction. She chewed slowly, incessantly, with a rhythmic side-to-side movement that evoked memories of my grandfather's barnyard. Every time I asked her to schedule a patient's return visit, she said, "I'll see what I can do." Twenty times a day, a hundred times a week, five thousand times a year—and without letting up on her chewing for an instant—she said, "I'll see what I can do."

Despite her perseverance and dour placidity, Mildred remembered the names and birth dates of all the patients in our clinic, and every day she read the obituary section of the *Louisville Courier-Journal*. Before she came to work for us, we often suffered the embarrassment of calling an elderly gentleman's home to find out why he had missed an appointment or refused to pay his bill, only to discover that the poor fellow was lying in Cave Hill Cemetery. Thanks to Mildred, every week or two I would find a chart lying on my desk with *DECEASED* printed across the cover in Mildred's perfect hand, block letters like those in the workbooks of grade-school children. On most occasions, she taped an obituary clipped from the *Louisville Courier-Journal* beneath this label.

One patient in particular comes to mind. Michael Harvey, a handsome, broad-shouldered fellow, was under my care for ocular histoplasmosis. Since he was only forty-nine and, except for his eye disease, had seemed in good health during a visit some weeks before, I was startled to find his chart lying on my desk with *DECEASED* printed across the cover. The usual obituary was missing, so I asked Mildred if she knew how he had died.

"Oh, yes," she said. "It was on the news last night. They showed four patrol cars pulled up in Mr. Harvey's driveway."

"What happened?" I asked.

"His wife beat him to death with a pipe wrench."

"Beat him to death with a pipe wrench! Why the hell did she do that?"

"'Cause he was a plumber," she replied. Her placid face showing no trace of a smile.

* * *

Ophthalmology is a dangerous specialty. If medical students spend one day amidst our marvelous array of gadgets, even the most jaded and worldly wise among them might fall under our spell. Yes, urologists and cardiologists have their toys, and proctologists use some fancy endoscopes, but these are mere trifles compared to what one finds in the offices and operating rooms of ophthalmologists. We have slit-lamp microscopes, optical miracles whose narrow beams slice deep into the eye's glittering layers: corneal endothelium, lens capsule, iris crypts and ruffs, diaphanous vascular nets that weave their way through the retina and choroid and optic nerve. Our lasers flash pinpoint bursts of energy, reshaping tissues to tolerances no wider than a human hair. Wafer-thin knives peel away scars, while instruments smaller than a pencil lead suck up blood, vitreous gel, and emulsified lens material, clearing the visual axis and restoring sight to hundreds of thousands of patients every year.

Yet despite such marvelous devices, the blind are still with us—blind men, blind women, and blind children. To sustain my sanity, I learned to harden my heart. Which is to say, I seldom wept with the men and women who just learned from my lips that they would never read or drive again. Yet beyond the usual maladies—diabetic retinopathy, macular degeneration, the all-but-endless array of eye diseases that afflict adults—my practice held for me one special terror.

At long intervals, perhaps two or three times a year, that terror stalked me down. Mildred would touch my sleeve as I passed her desk, then whisper in my ear, "There's a kid waiting for you in Lane 1. It doesn't look good." Mildred's perspicacity was uncanny. A glance at a note from the referring ophthalmologist or a conversation overheard in the waiting room was enough to set her curious mind aflame. In Lane 1, I would find an innocent, smooth-skinned boy or girl. They may have been five or six years old. They may have been ten or twelve. Often the visits came in late August or early September, during the first week of school—a classroom filled with unfamiliar objects.

The teacher had observed an odd behavior, an exceptional clumsiness that—coming on slowly, as these dreaded things always do—had escaped the parents' notice. The child who stumbled was anxious, fearful of a strange doctor. The parent accompanying the child, almost always the mother, showed in her face and voice a deeper fear. The ophthalmologist who referred the child to me had already aroused the first stirrings of terror: "It could be...no, no, we're not certain, of course...but it could be..." This was not the common and hoped-for myopia or astigmatism, disorders easily remedied with spectacles.

Often the child was so small he must kneel in my examination chair to lift his tiny face up to my slit-lamp microscope. Under the lamp's slender beam, his corneas would be crystal clear—no trace of opacity, no clouding of the anterior chamber, no hemorrhage in the vitreous gel. The problem lay deeper, far back in the eye, where the retina of a healthy child gleams and glitters like polished glass. But not in this child. Here there was only dullness, a terrible wasting that announced its onset with ragged black strands—a pattern textbooks describe as "bone spicules." The normal pastel shades of coral and sienna and burnt umber had vanished, replaced by mottled patches of decayed retina, stealing, in the end, the last ray of light from the child's visual field.

Retinitis pigmentosa. Mildred had scored another hit. I would take a deep breath, hold the child's thin arm as he climbed down from the exam chair, send him to the play room, and then explain to the mother that a fragment of genetic code had faltered, a defect beyond the most powerful microscope, and now strands of corrosive rot had destroyed her son's vision. A molecular mistake, and now those delicate retinal tissues—a hundred million rods and cones, a billion axons and dendrites and glial cells, joined in a matrix of wondrous complexity—had begun a hopeless downward spiral. The child stumbled because his vision had shrunk to a tiny island in a sea of darkness.

How long before he would become totally blind? It could be years. Three, maybe five. Or it could be...

* * *

When I was ten years old, my neighborhood gang dug its way into an abandoned septic tank. It gave off a horrid stench, but more terrible yet were the sounds we heard when our shovel broke through the rusted cover—a bubbling, belching rumble as the noxious gas escaped. Our prize was the hideous black mess at the bottom of the pit, a mess so awful we came back again and again to look. One night, flashlight in hand, we convinced ourselves we could see giant worms wriggling beneath the slime. To this day, the image sends a thrill of revulsion down my spine.

Later in life, I would discover revulsions that brought not a childish thrill but heart-thumping terror. Anatomy lab, for example. From the moment I was accepted to medical school, the thought of dissecting a cadaver made my pulse race. I reassured myself with the neurotic's classic mantra—"Calm down, you fool, things never turn out as badly as you imagine"—but when the day finally came, I found myself stumbling through a nightmare more terrible than the one I had feared.

Late afternoon. An ancient stone-walled building. A long, dim corridor lined on both sides by tables, each table covered by a white plastic sheet whose telltale bumps betray the contour of a corpse laid upon its back. The reek of formaldehyde stings my eyes. My knees wobble. My heart flops wildly in my chest. A surge of nausea fills my throat with bile.

Medical students dissect cadavers in order to learn human anatomy, but this is at best a secondary purpose. The first law of medical decorum states that a doctor must not faint dead away when he encounters a gaping wound or a festering rectal abscess, and pedagogy has yet to discover better assurance against such an event than twelve months spent peeling every fragment of tissue from an embalmed corpse. Formaldehyde turns muscles grey, while skin takes on the color of liverwurst. The fecal contents of the colon and small bowel retain their signature bouquet. Embalming remains an imperfect science, allowing bacteria to putrefy the glistening yellow fat that erupts from the abdominal cavity. Compared to the rancid cadaver my lab partners and I dissected, a rectal abscess is a nosegay.

This gross-out treatment worked. After we had spent four months slicing our way up the lower extremities and deep into the pelvic cavity, my lab partners and I were battle-scarred veterans. We washed our hands before urinating rather than after, shed no tears to formaldehyde fumes, and worked through the lunch hour with two kibitzers munching ham sandwiches while their partners peeled away malodorous strips of paraspinous muscle to expose the knobby white spine. Steve Baird, one of my partners, insisted he could dine, twitching nary an eyebrow, from a plate laid in our cadaver's gaping abdominal cavity.

The anatomy lab served its purpose. By the time we had stripped away the last sinew, leaving only a skeleton, a gangrenous appendix caused me no more distress than a fly squashed on a windowpane. I did not tremble or flee the emergency room when a gush of blood splashed on my shoes. In the operating room, if fumes escaped from a putrid colonic pocket, my stomach heaved and my brow grew damp with sweat, but I did not faint.

By the third year of medical school, blood and gore posed no problem, but one evening in the ER, while watching a resident sew up a split lip, my machismo collapsed. The patient, a tall, willowy high school student, had been beaten and raped. It wasn't the wound that did me in, the tiny stitches or drops of blood from each needle puncture, but the victim's soft, rhythmic sobs—sobs that spoke of a hideous violation. One moment I was peering over the resident's shoulder, puzzled by a strange weakness in my legs, the next moment I was sitting on the floor with my head tucked between my knees. An orderly had eased my slumped body against a wall to keep me from cracking my head. Sweat soaked the armpits of my blue scrub shirt. My heart was hardened against wounds of the flesh, but nothing I had seen in the lab or the lecture hall could prepare me for the revulsion of forced penetration.

* * *

Retinitis pigmentosa—the words have a raspy, unpleasant feel on the tongue. They speak of ineluctable blindness, of a child's world shrinking to a tiny, vanishing point. And they offer a special shock to the mother who accompanies the child. Are you and the father blood relatives? If so— if you succumbed to your cousin's wealth, or his charm, or his husky bedroom voice—then mark against yourself a charge of contributory negligence. Retinitis pigmentosa is often inherited as a recessive disorder. To suffer its ravages, the unlucky victim must receive a defective gene from both parents, an especially common event when that child is born of a consanguineous union. Thus the innocent bear the curse of their own conception.

Nor is blindness the end of the story. On occasion, retinitis pigmentosa brings a vile cousin of its own, the Usher syndrome, first described in 1858 by Albrecht Von Gräfe, a pioneer of modern ophthalmology. Here a genetic defect erodes not only the child's retinas but his cochleas as well, allowing deafness to ride upon the shoulders of blindness. Over time, the victim's world vanishes beneath a black and silent sea, leaving behind only what he can touch, taste, or smell.

* * *

Classicists have long argued that beauty's true foundation rests on the union of form with function. Which is to say, those natural structures that accomplish their tasks with grace and efficiency are invariably beautiful to behold. In support of this notion, the ancient Greeks covered their landscape with statues of naked men and women. I've always found this notion a bit dodgy. However lovely the nubile female form, the wrinkly, pendulous genitals of your typical male—as seen in a shower or a locker room, rather than on the sculpted fantasies of Athens—strike me as an aesthetic disaster. And few would find visual pleasure in a mass of churning intestines, no matter how efficiently they digested a meal.

I will concede one point to the classicists: though a well-functioning organ may or may not be beautiful, disease is always ugly. Tumors, ulcers, and necrotic flesh are the most hideous things on earth. And there is a distance to be measured—measured in units of horror and revulsion—between the loveliness of a healthy eye and the blinding rot that destroys it, a distance that separates the azure sky of a summer day from the bottom of the pit. And yet, as I discovered near the end of my career, the ultimate horror comes not from nature, even at her worst, but from the willful hand of man.

* * *

Lila Summers. The name still troubles me. Would that I had been spared Lila, or better yet, that she had been spared her destiny. In clinic one afternoon, a few months before I assumed the comfortable part-time role of professor emeritus, Mildred gave me her somber warning: "Doctor Gamel, I think we've got another one." I wasn't in the mood to listen. Her previous warnings had missed the mark when one patient suffered from a benign retinopathy that resembled retinitis pigmentosa but had little effect on vision. Another patient, an eight-year-old malingerer, had feigned blindness to lure his parents' affection away from a newborn baby brother.

I was also distracted by the apparent cheerfulness of Lila's mother, a slender young woman whose pale skin bore no trace of makeup. An auburn pageboy framed her narrow face. She seemed a girl herself, too young to be the mother of a twelve-year-old, but the dreadful meaning of this fact didn't dawn on me until later in the day. The two made a fetching pair, more like sisters than mother and daughter. Both wore simple white shifts trimmed at hem and sleeve with a double row of cornflowers. Lila carried her right arm in a cast slung about her shoulder. Her right ankle was bound with an elastic bandage. She limped as she entered my office and climbed into the exam chair.

The mother's voice showed no hint of the anxiety I had come to expect in such cases, allowing the story she told to creep up on my blind side. She gazed steadily into my eyes. A smile flickered at the corners of her mouth, as though she hoped I would find her tale amusing. Only too late did I discover the truth: what I saw in her face was not humor or cheerfulness but the desperation of a woman-child begging me to laugh at her foolish, misguided fears.

"It's so silly," she said, patting Lila on the knee. "Ridiculous, if you ask me. Lila's drama teacher said I should bring her to an eye doctor. She was there, she saw Lila fall. They were practicing *The Nutcracker Suite* with the lights turned down so these glow-in-the-dark sparkles on the wings of the sugarplum fairies would show up better. It wasn't all that dark, the other kids got around fine, but Lila fell into the orchestra pit."

The mother leaned forward to touch my wrist, then caught herself. She smiled, giggled, shook her head from side to side to show her exasperation. Her smile said, *How absurd.* She crossed her legs and smoothed her skirt. She giggled again. Her smile pleaded, *Tell me she's wrong, Doctor. Please tell me the teacher's wrong.*

As her story unfolded, my heart sank. I told myself to buck up, stop being such a pessimist, but when I examined Lila's eyes—there it was. Her retinas had withered to tiny spots, spots that would soon vanish beneath a ragged black tide. I took a deep breath, forced a smile, and sent Lila from the room. I needed more information before unloading this nightmare on the mother.

"Is your daughter hard of hearing?"

"Well...yes...maybe a little..."

"OK, OK," I said, holding up my hand to stop her voice. At that moment, on that subject, I had all the information I could handle. I scribbled a note in the chart. "We'll refer Lila to an audiologist. My receptionist will take care of it. Just a few more questions. Are you and your husband related by blood?"

The mother hesitated. She looked at me. Her face—again, there was something I couldn't read. Not a frown, certainly not a smile. Confusion? Anxiety?

"You and your husband," I said, "are you first or second cousins, anything like that?"

"No," she said at last. "We couldn't be related. He's from California, I met him when he was in basic training at Fort Knox. Nobody else in his family has ever come anywhere near Kentucky."

Perhaps I had asked the wrong question, but never mind. I didn't say, "In five years, your beautiful daughter will be blind as a stone and maybe deaf to boot." No, I said, "We'll need more tests to be sure, but I suspect your daughter's vision is failing because of an inherited disease, a disease she was born with. It may take many years before.... We can't be sure when..."

As the truth dawned in the mother's widening eyes, she clutched my arm and pressed the other hand against her mouth. I patted her knee, offered a box of tissues, and waited through long, terrible minutes of choking sobs. Then came the usual litany—"Can't you do something, Doctor? You mean there's no treatment, nothing at all?"—repeated two or three times, her voice quavering between incredulity and anger. At last she fell silent. Her nose and cheeks remained fiery red, but her eyes were dry. I walked her to the appointment desk with my arm across her narrow shoulders, then bucked myself up to examine my last ten or twelve patients. Finally—exhausted, dispirited, eager for my impending retirement—I strode through the empty waiting room and snatched open the door to the parking lot.

Mildred sat alone at her desk, stolid and mountainous as ever. I had passed without noticing her. She shouted at me from across the empty room.

"Doctor Gamel, that woman, Lila Summers' mother, she said I should tell you something."

I propped the door open with my foot and turned back toward her desk.

"What?" I shouted back.

"She didn't want to tell you herself, said she felt too nervous."

Mildred sounded nervous herself, her usual monotone giving way to a raucous shout, loud even across the empty room. Very annoying.

"Tell me what?"

"It was her father. She was twelve."

"What?" I asked.

"Her father was the one."

My God, what was that idiot going on about? The charts I carried under my arm had to be stacked on my desk before I could meet my wife for dinner, and the next day I had an appointment with our department's new chairman, who might reject the retirement contract I had negotiated with the old chairman. The last thing I needed was Mildred's nonsense.

I said "Thanks," then let the door slam behind me. Halfway home it struck me. I pulled my car off the road into a service station. It took me a long time to collect my thoughts. Finally, the attendant shouted at me to move if I wasn't going to buy gas.

* * *

Lila's audiology tests revealed marginal loss in the higher frequencies but no definite abnormality. Thus, with a little luck, she would someday hear the laughter of her grandchildren. At my retirement, soon after her appointment, I turned her care over to our new chairman, a world-renowned retinal specialist whose skills, like mine, could offer not the slightest hope of extracting the cruel seed planted in every cell of Lila's body. During the years since my retirement, he has told me nothing about her progress, and I have chosen not to ask.

CHAPTER SEVENTEEN

Mother Nature and Father Time

If we live long enough, our eyes will always fail us. Most ten-year-olds can count the legs on an ant, while only the rare hundred-year-old can see the ant itself. Mother Nature is a bitch, Father Time is a son of a bitch, and sooner or later our eyes—along with our knees, hearts, and hair—will surrender to this vile duo. During the early years of life, the sclera is snowy white, the ocular media—composed of the cornea, lens, and vitreous gel—remain crystal clear, while the retina shimmers and shines under the light of an ophthalmoscope. Indeed, the sparkle we see in children's eyes is no illusion. But during our twenties, the shank of young adulthood, the luster begins to fade, foreshadowing the greenish cataract and rheumy yellow sclera of senescence.

Old age launches its first assault on our crystalline lens, a lentil-shaped tissue that hangs behind the iris, suspended by a thousand translucent filaments. Tension on these filaments allows youngsters to focus their eyes from near to far with the ease and precision of a Nikon camera, but to sustain its marvelous clarity, the lens must survive without capillaries, nourished only by the oxygen-poor aqueous.

Such metabolic tenuousness leaves the lens vulnerable to every biological assault. Like the canary in the mine, it is often the first tissue to suffer when exposed to radiation, toxins, or aging. As we enter our fifth decade, our lenses begin to lose their elasticity, bringing the curse of bifocals or reading glasses. Then, inexorable as an unloved season, cataracts appear, diffracting light into haloes, casting an odd tint on familiar objects, finally drawing a dark veil over our world.

If Granddaddy lives long enough, he won't be able to read, but if he's lucky—if cataracts are the only cause of his impairment—twenty minutes at the hands of a skilled surgeon, and the opaque lump is gone, sucked out through a vibrating needle and replaced by an acrylic lens the size of a cornflake. The next morning, Granddaddy will pore over his morning newspaper with the alacrity of a youngster.

* * *

"It's macular degeneration, isn't it, Doctor?"

"Yes, I'm afraid so."

To see clearly, we need more than a clear cornea and a clear lens. Much more: a tissue that transforms light into nervous impulses, an optic nerve to transmit these impulses to the brain, and a visual cortex to process the impulses. The first link in this chain is the retina, a delicate, multilayered, altogether wondrous membrane.

But alas, the retina, like the lens, must sooner or later surrender to Mother Nature and Father Time.

As we live beyond our sixth decade, an ever-increasing number of us will suffer from macular degeneration, a disease that affects the macula, or central portion of the retina. Here live the densely packed cells that provide our sharpest vision. Age begins its evil work by dissolving the silvery sheen that adorns the retinas of the young. Then, as time passes, our eyes descend into the ragged wasteland known as "dry" macular degeneration, an insidious progress akin to the wrinkles and liver spots that transform a baby's face into the face of a crone. Year by year, line by line on the acuity chart, the victim's vision fails, stealing her ability to drive or read the printed word.

* * *

"Doctor, when I got up this morning, there was a big spot in my right eye. It blocks out everything I look at."

This was Sister Maria, an eighty-four-year-old nun. I have heard similar complaints from a sixty-nine-year-old railroad engineer and an eighty-six-year-old retired prizefighter with a crooked nose. A colleague of mine, a professor at the Louisville Medical School, spoke more bluntly. One afternoon he got up from his desk in the Pathology Department, walked across Muhammad Ali Boulevard, and barged into my clinic.

"Dammit, Gamel," he said, "what the hell's going on with my right eye?"

The moment I heard their complaints, I knew these were the unlucky ones. Most patients with macular degeneration have the dry form, which steals vision slowly, but some suffer an abrupt hemorrhage or leakage beneath the retina that marks the onset of the "wet" form. From that point on, every object they look at disappears into a black hole. Fate makes only one concession: though the blind spot tends to enlarge over time, and though it almost always destroys the ability to read or drive, it rarely obliterates all sight, allowing most victims to navigate a familiar environment.

"Doctor...please...tell me...is there a treatment?"

Dry-eyed or weeping, motionless or wringing their hands, clear-voiced or choked with fear, sooner or later every patient with macular degeneration will ask the same question. Theory offers two potential cures: transplanting the eye or replacing the retina and its supporting structures. For the moment, both procedures remain well beyond the reach of science. The complexity of the retina rivals that of the brain itself. To transplant either organ, the surgeon must reconnect millions of axons—microscopic neural tubes so fragile the subtlest trauma destroys them forever. I suspect this achievement will elude the best surgeons for generations to come.

At the moment, we can boast little progress against dry macular degeneration. The only proven remedy is a regimen of vitamins and antioxidants that delays—but does not stop—the insidious loss of vision. On a more positive note, recent advances in molecular research have given us a panoply of new drugs for treating wet macular degeneration. Though vastly more effective than the therapies available early in my career, these agents remain an imperfect cure. They must be injected into the eye repeatedly, they improve vision in only a minority of patients, and of these, only a lucky few sustain the improvement for the remainder of their lives. Despite the triumphs of modern medicine, decay is written into our genes. It is our destiny.

*　*　*

Boris Osterhaus was a grey-haired farmer from Cecelia, Kentucky. His potbelly stretched the bib of his denim overalls. Minutes after arriving in my office, he pulled a pouch of Red Man Chewing Tobacco from his pocket, then, realizing this was neither the time nor the place to tuck a wad into his cheek, he grimaced and stuffed the pouch back in his pocket. An optometrist in Cecelia had referred him to an ophthalmologist in Elizabethtown, the ophthalmologist had referred him to me, and now, after a hundred miles over backcountry roads, Boris learned from my lips that he would never read or drive again. A dry, pockmarked wilderness had destroyed the macula in both of his eyes. When I finished my spiel—a diplomatic version of "Mother Nature is a bitch, Father Time is a son of a bitch, and there's not a damn thing I can do about it"—Boris leapt from his chair to grip me in a knuckle-cracking handshake.

"Thank you, Doctor, thank you so much. I just can't tell you how good it is to finally hear the truth straight up and down. Now I can get that confounded woman"—he gestured toward the stern-faced daughter who had brought him—"to stop dragging me all over the county. She keeps saying nowadays you doctors can fix anything. What a load of rubbish! I've lived eighty-three hard-bitten years, and ain't nobody in my family been able to read much after they was seventy-five or eighty. That's just the way it is. I knew it all along, but she wouldn't listen."

* * *

Of all my patients with macular degeneration, Hans Bergerman proved the most astute observer. This was no surprise, given his curriculum vitae: professor emeritus, former chairman of Stanford's Department of Anthropology, editor of five books, and author of 200 academic publications. His bushy brows and bald, sun-darkened head gave him a gnomish look. Born in Brazil of German parents, he spoke with a crisp accent and sat stiff as a soldier in the exam chair. He never took his eyes off me for a moment.

"Let's see how this matches yours," he said, handing me a sketched outline of the distorted spot he had discovered in his right eye. I was drawing my own picture of the lesion that lurked beneath the macula of that eye. Both drawings resembled a childish doodle of a wolf's head, but in my doodle the snout and ears were done with a red pencil to show streaks of subretinal blood. The wolf's bulbous jowl was formed by a tangle of pathologic vessels that threatened to hemorrhage at any moment, destroying Bergerman's central vision forever. The diagnosis was obvious—wet macular degeneration. Several years before, the same disease had destroyed the central vision in his left eye.

Bergerman was lucky. Wet macular degeneration usually strikes in the central portion of the retina, where laser therapy—the only option available at that time— would cause instant blindness. When I saw that his lesion lay a fraction of a millimeter removed from the center, I felt a shiver of anxiety. It was my task to treat the poor man by cauterizing the tangle of vessels with a laser beam, though the zone that divided success from disaster was no greater than the width of a few human hairs. Doug Jacobson, who watched my every move through the slit-lamp microscope attached to the laser, would never know how much sweat dripped from my armpits as I fired dozens of blue-green flashes into Bergerman's eye.

Three months later, Bergerman said, "Thank you, Doctor." His vision was 20/30. The tangle of vessels had shrunk to a dry, flat scar. He thanked me again two years later, the day he awoke to find his central vision obliterated by a huge blind spot. My treatment had failed. I knew it would fail—unless the patient died first, treatment of macular degeneration during that era always failed—but my heart sank at the sight of that dark clot beneath his retina.

"Thank you very much," he said. "You allowed me to read for an extra two years." While leaving the exam room, he stopped to shake my hand and give my shoulder a friendly squeeze. With a rueful smile, he said, "You sound so sad, Doctor, like you just lost your best friend. Who do you think you are—a magician, a god who makes old men young forever?"

* * *

I am now eight years into the final phase of my career. As advised by a wise senior colleague, I have chosen to consider myself "repotted" rather than "retired." Whatever the terminology, I have given up full-time practice. Now I lecture to my residents, staff a few clinics every month, and write the story of my life.

As my dotage approaches, I am happy to report that my lifelong attack on hypochondria has proved a success. Over the years, as I faced down my fear, the anxieties became less frequent and less severe. Now a stomach pain or a sore on my skin brings only a twinge of the old fear. Perhaps my hypochondria faded over time thanks to aging, the same villain that has stolen much of my hair, libido, and skin turgor. But no, I reject this theory. Nor do I accept such unheroic, mealy mouthed terms as "desensitization" or "self-actualization." I like to think that raw courage affected my cure, that my suffocating phobias gave way to a bold, headlong assault. It makes a better story.

But life has played a trick on me. My fear of death—the enemy I kept at bay by racing headlong into a medical career—has returned, and my old weapons no longer work. My stoutest sword was the fact that healthy young men seldom keel over dead. This became my talisman, a mantra I chanted a dozen times a day to ward off irrational fears, but now a strange thing has happened: I am no longer young.

And yet, though I have grown wrinkled and half-bald, drawing closer to the grave with every breath, my life remains a sweet and precious thing. We humans are more than the sum of our failing parts. The wisest among us know that life cannot be cured, but we need someone to inform us and—when healing fails—to accompany us on the lonely road to blindness and death. I did not learn this truth in a book, a laboratory, or a lecture hall. My patients taught it to me. They came in desperation, returned year after year to share their struggles, and then, in the fullness of time, they died. One way or the other, I always lost the battle, but they gave me many precious moments.

The eye begins as a perfect thing, a miraculous organ, but its luster, mortal and doomed as life itself, fades with each passing year. I watched it all through my slit-lamp microscope. I watched my patients grow old with grace by facing down their fears, and slowly, decade by decade, they taught me how to do it.

About the Author

John Gamel was born and raised in Selma, Alabama, then obtained his BA from Harvard and his MD from Stanford. After additional training at Stanford and at the Armed Forces Institute of Pathology in Washington, DC, he moved to Louisville, Kentucky, in 1977. Here he became a professor of Ophthalmology at the University Of Louisville School Of Medicine, where he remained until his partial retirement in 2001. His scientific contributions include ninety-three articles that range in their subjects from fingerprints to breast cancer. He has published fifteen personal essays in a variety of literary journals, including *Epoch*, *Boulevard*, *The Antioch Review*, and *The Alaska Quarterly Review*. His work titled "The Elegant Eyeball" was included in *The Best American Essays 2010*.